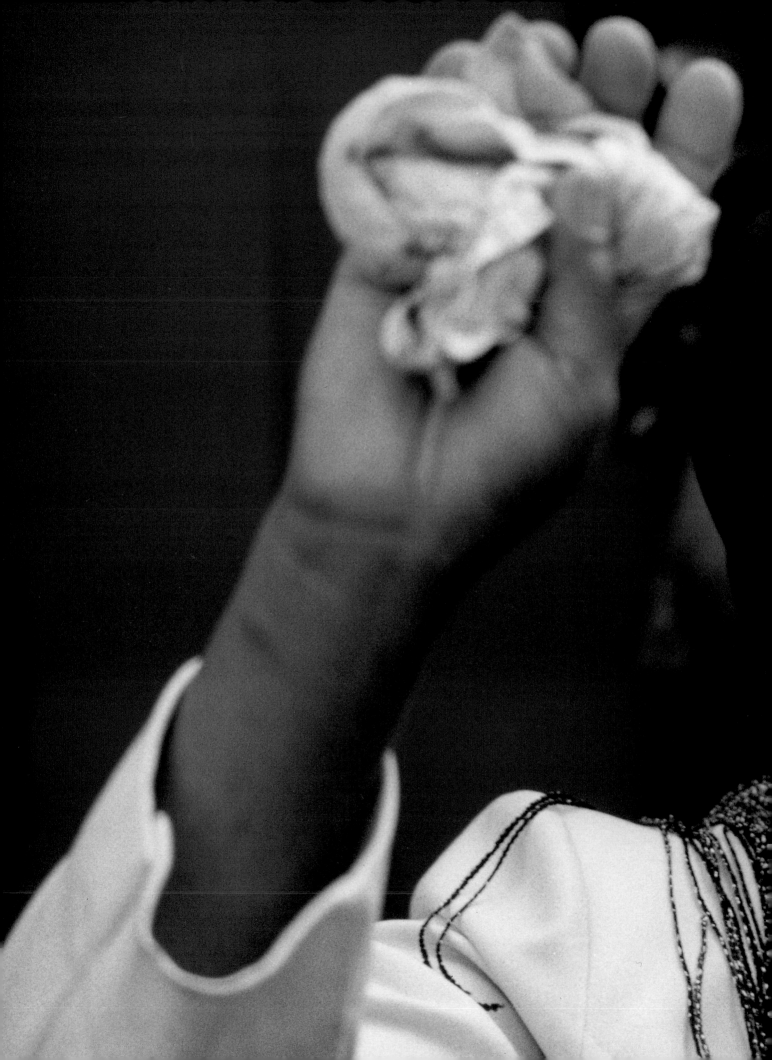

Why Are They Weeping?
South Africans under Apartheid

Photographs by David C. Turnley

Text by Alan Cowell

Foreword by Allan Boesak

Stewart, Tabori & Chang
New York

South Africa has been swept by a firestorm of activism since 1984. The unvarying state response has been repression and the opposition rallying point the funeral. In a country where outdoor political gatherings have been forbidden since 1976, mass burials became the heavily charged focus of grief, defiance, and politicization. Frequently, the police and army have intervened, resulting in yet another round of mourning and violence.

Page 1: Cape Town.

Pages 2 and 3: The Athlone area of Cape Town.

Pages 4 and 5: Mamelodi township, outside Pretoria.

Pages 6 and 7: Umlazi township, in Natal.

Pages 8 and 9: Alexandra township, in Johannesburg.

Pages 10 and 11: Duncan Village, outside East London.

Frontispiece: In a solitary moment before a mass funeral, a woman mourns her brother, killed by riot police in a township near George.

Library of Congress Cataloging-in-Publication Data

Turnley, David C.

   Why are they weeping? : South Africans under apartheid / photographs by David C. Turnley : text by Alan Cowell.

   1. Apartheid—South Africa. 2. Apartheid—South Africa—Pictorial works. I. Cowell, Alan. II. Title.

DT763.5.T88   1988

968.06′3—dc19   88-14101

ISBN 1-55670-044-X (cloth)
     1-55670-054-7 (paper)

Published in 1988 by Stewart, Tabori & Chang, Inc.
740 Broadway, New York, New York 10003
Distributed by Workman Publishing,
708 Broadway, New York, NY 10003

The publisher and photographer gratefully acknowledge support from the Eastman Kodak Company in the publication of this book.

Captions by Miriam Lacob.
Design by Jeff Batzli.
Printed in Japan.
88 89 90 91 92 9 8 7 6 5 4 3 2 1

ACKNOWLEDGMENTS

There are many people whose support and friendship I would like to acknowledge.

My dream to make this book began when Vice President and General Manager, Professional Photography Division of the Eastman Kodak Company Raymond DuMoulin pledged his company's support after seeing a presentation of my work in Arles, France, during the summer of 1987.

The *Detroit Free Press* made an extraordinary commitment by keeping me in South Africa for two and a half years. I want to thank all of my colleagues at the *Free Press*, and, in particular: publisher David Lawrence, Jr.; executive editor Heath Meriwether; Kent Bernhard; Assistant Managing Editor/Graphics Randy Miller and his wife Linda; Tony Spina; Marcia Prouse; Sandra White; Bill Roberts; Joe Ricci; John Goecke; Mike Smith; Pat Beck; Bob McKean; Helen McQuerry; and Diane Bond. Working with *Free Press* African correspondent Larry Olmstead was an immense pleasure both personally and professionally.

Perhaps the greatest credit—in the creation of this book, and for his ever-present integrity and commitment to photojournalism—goes to Howard Chapnick, president of Black Star. Also at Black Star I want to particularly thank Howard's lovely wife of forty-two years, Jeanette; Yukiko Launois; and the rest of the Black Star family.

A significant number of photographs in this book were the result of a story on the Afrikaners for the *National Geographic* magazine. Special thanks to the magazine's editor, Wilbur E. Garrett; senior assistant editor and director of photography Tom Kennedy; and assistant director of illustrations Rob Hernandez.

For their support of my work in South Africa, thanks to Karen Mullarkey, picture editor at *Newsweek*; *Life* director of photography Peter Howe and former director John Loengard; Picture Editor Bobbi Baker Burrows; Christopher Whipple; and *Time*'s Arnold Drapkin.

I had the pleasure of working in South Africa with many wonderful colleagues, only some of whose names I will mention: Peter Magubane; William Campbell; Mark Peters; Louise Gubb; Greg English; Patrick Nagel; Amy Reichert; Richard Sergay.

I was blessed during my tenure in South Africa to be exposed to South Africans across the ethnic and political spectrum who opened their doors to me to photograph their lives. Many of these people taught me much about the meaning of faith and courage. I want to particularly thank Mrs. Winnie Mandela; Archbishop Desmond Tutu and his wife Leah; Dr. Allan Boesak and his wife Dorothy; Andre Brink; Dr. Frederick Van Zyl Slabbert; Marie Botha; Jan and Annette Coetzee; the Andrew Louw family; Puleng; my friends at the Carlton Hotel; and countless others.

I have had the good fortune of working with Stewart, Tabori and Chang. Starting with publisher Andy Stewart, everyone at this publishing house has embraced the project. It has been a pleasure to work with Maureen Graney, the editor of the book. One rarely finds the kind of professionalism and commitment she has given this project. Thanks to Alan Cowell for his insightful writing and to Dr. Allan A. Boesak for his foreword, which I cherish. And thanks to Karen Branan for her help.

Finally, I want to thank Karin, my parents, my brothers Bill and Peter, and my sister Ann, for their love and for sharing in my dream.
        —David C. Turnley

Contents

16 Foreword
by Allan Boesak

19 Preface
by David C. Turnley

24 State of Emergency: South Africa 1985 to . . .
by Alan Cowell

56 Photographs
by David C. Turnley

Foreword

I T WAS SHAKESPEARE IN *HENRY V* WHO proclaimed the desire for an art form that had been an eternal dream until modern times: "O, for a Muse of fire that would transcend the highest heaven of invention!" In photography, human inventiveness has fashioned such an art form. The blink of an eye— the time for a camera shutter to snap—and the lightning stroke of history is captured. Triumphs and tragedies, epic events and private moments: there are no human endeavors or emotions that do not live forever through the skill of an ingenious photographer. David Turnley is such a photographer.

Good pictures, of course, do not come out of a vacuum. Colorful personalities, dramatic events, and extraordinary scenes are the elements needed. Certainly for a photographer, the beauty and tragedy of South Africa offers a compelling canvas from which to work. The land of apartheid—the official government policy of the separation of races, white domination, and economic exploitation—is a place of mounting turmoil. A white minority, descendants of European conquerors, presses on with its plan to uproot the native people—80 percent of the population—from our ancestral homes and to relocate us in bleak, arid "homelands" that comprise 13 percent of the country's land. For black people, the African Indian, and so-called coloured (mixed race) people, the daily grind of oppression ranges from discrimination and poverty to wholesale murder at the hands of state police and a mighty army. Any form of dissent is ruthlessly oppressed, and basic human rights are as alien to the landscape as life-giving water is to the desert. A people cry out, "How long, Lord?" A concerned humanity hears this cry. Some, like David Turnley, have come to this place to aid the oppressed with their struggle.

The photographs in this volume represent a pictorial essay of the States of Emergency imposed upon our people by the Pretoria regime. David Turnley was on the scene with his camera during the eventful years from 1985 to 1987. I began to notice Turnley at political rallies, mass funerals, government protests, church services, prayer vigils, and marches. He was everywhere. His drive to get a picture might be considered bravado or recklessness, but he always got the job done, usually vividly.

I remember one horrifying afternoon, and his role. I was presiding over the funeral of an innocent boy who had been shot dead by the police. The angry and bitter crowd turned murderous when they discovered an alleged police informer in their midst. I have no respect for police informers, but when I saw the man dragged out of the church and beaten, I had to intervene to save his life. It was all I could do to tear him from the crowd's clutches. David Turnley was in front of me, madly photographing the scene. I shouted at him, "Get me a car! Get me a car!" He reached into his pocket with one hand, never lowering the camera from his face, gave me a ring of car keys, and pointed "It's the little blue Toyota over there!" Not once did he stop taking pictures! I escaped with the alleged informer and his two sisters in Turnley's car.

The years 1985–1987 were dangerous times. Indeed, the current times are no less dangerous. But David Turnley is no longer in South Africa. His permit to work here was revoked. Pretoria pursues a policy of covering up its dirty work from the world. Photographing scenes of conflict is now illegal, and police thugs at whim confiscate film, and smash the equipment, of photographers. Those who attempt to record ongoing events face danger every day—not from the crowds of the oppressed, who want their story told and who recognize the importance of the world press, but from a bullet fired from a police van or an army tank. It takes tremendous courage to work under those conditions. David Turnley's courage, as well as his skill, is evident in each frame presented in this volume. This book is a documentary. It is also a testimony to a photographer's dedication and a people's courage and determination.   —Allan Boesak

Preface

I STEPPED OUT OF MY CAB AND HANDED my bags to a tall, young, black porter as I arrived at the Carlton Hotel in modern downtown Johannesburg. He replied with his eyes glued to the ground, "Thank you, boss." This was my first introduction to the reality of apartheid in South Africa.

When we arrived at my room, I handed the man a tip and asked him his name. He seemed surprised, looking up for the first time. He timidly said his name was Ronald. I told him he should call me David.

Two and a half years later, Ronald and many of his black co-workers, who in many ways had become my family during the time I lived in that hotel, joined a farewell party in my honor. I had been asked to leave South Africa by the government for "biased photo material," and perhaps the most meaningful chapter of my life was coming to an end.

I first heard the word "apartheid" when I was in high school. My father had come home very depressed one evening. He recounted at the dinner table that he had picketed the local Rotary Club, which had invited two pro-apartheid South Africans to speak, and none of the Rotarians who had passed by his picket had understood the meaning of apartheid.

I first went to South Africa in July of 1985. Shortly after I arrived, President P. W. Botha delivered his notorious Rubicon speech in which he announced that South Africa would not be pushed around by the rest of the world and that his government would preserve the kind of privilege to which South African whites were accustomed. This meant that the major tenets of apartheid would not be scrapped for a long time.

During my first few months I traveled from one end of South Africa to the other, trying to cover one of the most intense periods of unrest in the country's history. But my objective was to document ordinary life, to humanize a situation that people understood only from headlines and news reports.

As a photojournalist, I was accepted in South Africa's townships where most of the country's urban blacks live. I was welcomed into homes and allowed to

FACING PAGE: *A woman and her child in their Soweto home.*

photograph moments of intimacy and moments of grief. There was a recognition that I meant well—that my purpose was to document the conditions there and the realities of being black in South Africa. I could not help being moved by the kind of treatment I received in the midst of a country where blacks are denied rights that I hold to be undeniable. I also could not help being moved by the strength, determination, and love that I felt in the middle of black funerals for youths who had been killed in these riots.

My own life in South Africa reflected the terrible split in that society. I would wake up early in the morning in a five-star hotel in the middle of a westernized, well-supplied, all-white city, and then travel to an all-black township some twenty to thirty miles away. There I would be in the middle of confrontations between blacks and South African police, or I would be photographing mass funerals for victims of those confrontations. It would be a shock to return again to the hotel where there was a world in which whites seemed oblivious to these realities. I will never forget Malcolm Pearce—an enlightened, English-speaking white architect—standing in his front yard in the serene all-white Cape Town suburb of Ronde-bosch, commenting that one would never know that ten minutes away exists a "coloured" township, Ath-lone, where it was difficult to breathe through the tear gas and where police had that week killed a number of protesting coloured youth.

By virtue of apartheid, South Africa has become a country divided into two worlds. What I learned was that I could move between the two worlds, and I was determined to document them.

Once I spent weeks in Henneman, a town in the Orange Free State, documenting an Afrikaner community. For seven days I lived on the Naudes' farm, and, like other families in their town, they had been good to me. They were warm, gracious, and hospitable people who reminded me in many ways of people in the midwestern United States, where I grew up.

The Naudes accepted me into their home and demanded only that I give them a fair shot in my coverage. Their family shared a love that was special, and in their community they are considered upstanding citizens and devoutly religious. And yet, while I could receive this kind of reception and trust as a white stranger, blacks who had worked on the farm for years, including those who helped to raise the children, had never been invited to share a meal.

It would be, however, too easy to portray the South African situation simplistically, as good versus bad, black versus white. I would be remiss not to mention the growing number of whites, in a country where dissent often has a painful price, who work toward a South Africa where all people can enjoy its fruits. What would be more fair would be to acknowledge how well apartheid has isolated whites in that country from the realities of blacks and how this isolation and ignorance has bred the fear that creates a formidable barrier to reconciliation. It is tragic in that both groups have an incredible love and pride for their country.

By the time of the 1986 press restrictions, which prohibited the photographing of "unrest," I was concentrating on life across the spectrum in South Africa. I worked on a series of photo essays on five families who represented the major ethnic groups in the country—black, so-called coloured, Indian, white English-speaking, and white Afrikaans-speaking. I also did photo essays on Archbishop Desmond Tutu and Winnie Mandela. During the last ten months of my stay I tried to document Afrikaner society and culture.

The press restrictions have been a hindrance in South Africa, but ultimately they will never stop the determination of photojournalists to cover that story. What the restrictions have certainly done is confirm to the world the South African government's understanding of the power of visual images.

—David C. Turnley

PAGES 22 AND 23: *The family of an Orange Free State farm laborer killed in a farm accident mourns his death.*

State of Emergency: South Africa 1985 to . . .

ABOVE ALL, IT WAS A TIME OF CHOICES. At Africa's tip, the fault lines shifted and people faced decisions that determined lives: whose side are you on, black or white? Do you want war or peace? Are you for the past with its twin demons of supremacy and indignity, or for a future of which one can only say: it will be different?

The choices were forced, not volunteered, by an upheaval of anger and revolt that started in September 1984 and continued for more than two years. The protesters' rocks confronted bullets and tear gas. The yearning among the black majority for change and power met with unprecedented white repression, expressed in a series of emergency decrees, first enforced in 1985, reimposed in 1986, and sharpened and refined until this day. These decrees struck at dissent, activism, and the residual freedom of the press.

When the turmoil eased in late 1986 and early 1987, it could almost have been argued that nothing, really, had changed despite the government's limited reforms. The white children still attended segregated schools in segregated suburbs, and the blacks went to theirs in the segregated townships with their blend of grit and misery. At birth, the children still registered according to race under the Population Registration Act—one of apartheid's sturdiest pillars—and, when the old folks died, they were laid to rest in cemeteries assigned to the dead according to race.

But no one in South Africa emerged unchanged from those years of confrontation. No one could honestly say that they had not been obliged, in some way, to reappraise their lives in the apartheid society and evaluate their readiness to accept or reject it.

Among the white minority, a fundamental shift had changed the equations of domestic politics. The old distinctions between English-speaking liberalism and Afrikaans-speaking conservatism had disappeared as more English-speakers, confused and looking for an anchor for the future, joined President P. W. Botha's National Party. Grasping for easy solutions to hard problems, many whites lurched collectively to the right, disregarding the agonies of conscience that settled on the few.

The relatively liberal Progressive Federal Party had been replaced as the official parliamentary opposition by the Conservative Party, an Afrikaner grouping looking to the old models of dominance and separation, rather than any new sense of sharing, as the means to extricate the country from inevitable tragedy.

Among the black majority, the battle lines sharpened more than ever, and the sullen quiescence that had followed the Soweto riots of 1976–77 fell away.

In some ways, too, black choices were more complex. Yes, a person might say, I want change; I want my people in power. But how would power be defined, and who would wield it? Was majority rule—whenever it came—to be qualified by special consideration of the white minority, as the Zulu Chief Mangosuthu Gatsha Buthelezi and his Inkatha movement proposed? Or was the demand for one-man, one-vote in a unitary society beyond negotiation, as the African National Congress (ANC) maintained from its position as the principal receptacle of black yearnings, the exiled and outlawed proponent of what it calls the "armed struggle" to unseat the minority regime?

For blacks and whites, in those years between 1984 and 1987, the violence of the protest and of the authorities' response sent the same message: choose, and choose now.

There were other grand issues, too, turning on the government's premise that the concept of ethnicity imparts its own legitimacy in what it sees as a fundamental struggle for white survival against the demonic possibility of black majority rule.

The men who run South Africa yearn for the appearance of legitimacy, which they create by juridical formulas that filter reality and cloak raw supremacy in the trappings of Western, constitutional behavior. The quasi-legalisms thus come to function in two ways: as a sinew of the rulers' power and as a display of affinity with those distant communities in Europe where rule of law is supposed to be paramount.

The protest of the mid-1980s tore the mantle of legitimacy apart. The urge to conjure what the authorities called constitutional change gave way to coercion and crackdown. Yet even repression had to be hidden in the legalistic contortions of the emergency decrees. To their critics, South Africa's white rulers would simply say that outsiders do not understand their country, that it is too complex, too "heterogeneous" for comprehension by those not born, raised, and steeped in it. But South Africa is no more complex than Lebanon, or West Germany, and probably far less complex than the United States. What is different is the way ethnic and racial complexity has been taken as the starting point for a political vision that denies and distorts demographic reality: in South Africa, more than most other places, an ideology has been implanted that the individual cannot escape from cradle to grave.

Repression is not unique to South Africa, as the country's rulers keep reminding those who criticize them. Many countries on earth are repressive and nasty, yet win the support of the democratic nations of the West, notably the United States, so there is a degree of hypocrisy in the opprobrium generated about Pretoria's policies. But institutionalized and constitutionalized repression rooted solely in race is South Africa's particular contribution to the current chronicles of authoritarianism that spell misery and fear for so many people, in black-ruled Africa, in parts of the Middle East, in Eastern Europe, and in much of what is called the Third World. With their hankering for identification with a community of nations both Christian and civilized, however, South Africa's rulers see themselves in a category different from the Stroessners and the Marcoses, the Khomeinis and the Saddam Husseins.

Their repression, they seem to be saying, is in a worthier cause, carried out under laws and decrees of their own enactment ostensibly supposed to resist Marxism and chaos and to offer salvation—not injustice—to what Pretoria calls the ethnic "nations" that form South Africa's patchwork.

By their own lights, the white rulers represent the West's distant outpost containing Soviet encroachment in Africa and therefore qualify for the West's support as much as Afghanistan's mujaheddin guerrillas or Nicaragua's contras. To their evident bafflement, support is withheld by a distant world perceived as living by double standards of morality and filled with people whose righteous indignation, as one government official once said, grows in direct proportion to the distance of its object from their own shores. The limited reforms the authorities enacted in the mid-1980s never seemed to be enough for an outside world baying for Pretoria's blood, the tacit support of the Reagan administration and of Prime Minister Margaret Thatcher of Britain notwithstanding.

Look, the authorities said, we have scrapped the hurtful laws barring marriage across color lines; there are nonwhites in our new parliament; the pass laws inhibiting black access to the peripheries of white cities have been repealed; there are racially mixed beaches in some places; there is, in short, a "new dispensation." What more do you want of us?

And the critics at home and abroad replied: of course the mixed marriages act has been scrapped, but where do those newlyweds across the color bar live when residential areas are still segregated; where do they send their children to school when schools are also still racially apportioned? And the argument continued: yes, there are nonwhites in the new parliament with its three racially distinct chambers, but they are Indians and so-called coloureds of mixed descent; there are no representatives of the black majority. The pass laws have gone, it is true, but now there is "orderly urbanization" that seems to serve a similar purpose in restricting black migration to the white-run cities. And, yes, they have taken away the "whites-only" sign at some beaches, but what about the many other amenities still segregated: the buses, the liquor stores, the beaches that remain racially apportioned?

We want more, the government's opponents said: we want an end to apartheid altogether, not a revised form of it cloaked as reform. What we want, they said—possibly ingenuously—is democracy, universal suffrage in a unitary state. If that is the case, the government responded, you are asking too much: you are asking for our surrender.

Beginnings

South Africa's National Party—the once-monolithic vehicle of Afrikaner aspirations—held no exclusive title to racial thinking when it came to power in 1948.

Across southern Africa, for decades of colonial rule, white authorities had imposed their will on blacks in various ways. In Northern and Southern Rhodesia, as Zambia and Zimbabwe were then called, blacks were supposed even to step off the sidewalk at the approach of a white. Colonial taxes, in South Africa and the region, had implanted the seeds of migratory labor by forcing men off the land and into mines whose wealth they did not share. Cities were divided into white "suburbs" and black "locations," as if black settlements merited no label other than strictly geographic. But South Africa's National Party had both a vision and the will to implant an ideology of ethnic separateness—between tribe and between shadings of skin color—that sought to legitimize the divide-and-rule tactics that European colonialism had enlisted more covertly when it created artificial boundaries elsewhere on the continent.

One explanation of what drove the Afrikaners, offered by some Afrikaners themselves, lay in the survival instincts of a tribe that saw no secure future if it did not build sharp boundaries protecting an identity created from religion, language, and race. But to the black majority and other nonwhites excluded from economic and political benefit, it was a political system built by whites to magnify individual greed, racism, and fear so that they became the basis of an entire society.

National Party power—rooted in the 2.8 million whites who trace their ancestry back to the Dutch settlement of the Cape in 1652 and who dominate South Africa's 4.5 million white population—was built with the same dogged resolve and organization as its black adversaries displayed many decades later. Since the 1930s, the party's ideological line had been formulated in the unchronicled conclaves of the ubiquitous Broederbond—formed in the early decades of this century as Afrikanerdom's secret society, from which the country's leaders were drawn—and had been given theological blessing in the teachings of the Dutch Reformed Church. Sentiments of oppression and resistance had been mobilized around such tribal festivals as the reenactment in 1938 of the Great Trek—the historic march inland from the Cape a century earlier—and the commemoration of battles and heroes at the huge stone monument outside Pretoria that provides the shrine of Africa's white tribe.

The National Party's ideological edifice was built on an interpretation of reality that starts from a dubious premise and proceeds logically from there. Once one accepts that South Africa is not a "homogeneous" society, then the rationale follows. If the land is made up of various "national groups" culturally and developmentally distinguished, on the one hand, by tribe and language and, on the other, by skin color, then it is unreasonable to suggest that they should all be ruled in the same way, or that one should be permitted to dominate the other by reason of numbers.

These arguments found legislative expression in the series of laws enacted by the National Party after it took power: the Population Registration Act and the Group Areas Act of 1950, the since-repealed Prohibition of Mixed Marriages Act of 1949, the Reservation of Separate Amenities Act of 1953, and the various items of legislation that inhibited black access to the segregated townships on the outskirts of white cities, the so-called pass laws that have now been replaced by other mechanisms to achieve the same purpose. Some of those laws merely tightened and refined legislation introduced in the early twentieth century by the British: the South Africa Act of 1909 barred blacks from parliament, the Natives Lands Act of 1913 established black reserves.

In the early 1980s, the edifice of apartheid, long challenged by the government's ideological adversaries, had begun to show strains from within as Afrikanerdom divided into a mainstream led by the National Party and a movement to its right, embodied in the Conservative Party of Dr. Andries Treurnicht. But those distinctions had little relevance for blacks.

The fires of the June 1976 Soweto uprising died a year later, replaced by a sullen anger and what, on the surface, seemed a generalized quiescence among the black majority. As late as October 1983, Ntatho Motlana, one of the leaders of the Soweto protest, was able to tell a newly arrived reporter that the South African Security Police had Soweto sewn up so tight with spies and informers that no one could breathe protest, let alone organize it. Yet the endless chronicles of modest personal sadnesses in that same brief calm showed as eloquently as the rocks and bombs that were to come how deeply apartheid's hurt had stained South Africa's fabric. The small stories that fell upon one another seemed, with hindsight, to be setting the stage for the sudden bursting of anger that swept away the resignation.

There was Eileen Giyani, for instance, a ten-year-old girl of mixed descent, whose parents had failed to register her at birth as a coloured and therefore she could not be lawfully categorized for a school. At first, she had gone to a segregated black school in Soweto but had been taunted there by other children for being of mixed race—exemplifying a twist in the nation's racial attitudes that is not usually acknowledged. Without the requisite documents, she could not register for a coloured school either. (The definition of a coloured person in the 1950 act is a person "who is neither a white person or a native," a classification derived solely from negatives.)

So she had found her way to the Good Shepherd Community Center, an unofficial school catering to those who had slipped through the web of classification that determines the entire lives of most South Africans. "The souls of the people," said Don Mateman, an organizer at the center, "have been killed by racism."

In Soweto, a forty-seven-year-old black woman,

Elder Olephant, had contrived to break one apartheid barrier only to run into another born of ingrained reflex rather than law. As a blind lawn bowls player, she said, she sometimes competed with blind white women players. Most of the players, she said, had been blind from birth, so had no chromatic notion of black or white. When the games were over, however, Mrs. Olephant said, the white women, helped by black maids, would ask their helpers to seat them among other whites at teatime. "They would say: 'keep me away from the Kaffirs,' " Mrs. Olephant recounted, smiling in her ruminative, sightless way.

The sense of stoic acceptance of the harsh realities of apartheid was not really surprising. Until Mr. Botha's "new dispensation" galvanized opposition there was, ironically, no apparent focus for protest. Nelson Mandela, the jailed leader of the ANC, remained incarcerated in Pollsmoor Prison near Cape Town, where he remains today, an untouchable figurehead silenced by more than two decades of incarceration. His wife, Winnie, was living in what amounted to internal exile, banned to the remote, black township near the Afrikaner town of Brandfort in the Orange Free State. The ANC itself, exiled in Zambia, Mozambique, and Angola, under Mandela's friend and asso-ciate Oliver Tambo, fought a desultory guerrilla war against Africa's most powerful military machine, striving to maintain its primacy as the standard-bearer of black yearnings, but not really denting the system. Within South Africa, activist priests such as Archbishop (then Bishop) Desmond M. Tutu and the Reverend Allan A. Boesak, Frank Chikane, and Bishop Simeon Nkoane spoke out frequently and eloquently against the system that overwhelmed millions of lives. But the catalyst that created the coalition of resistance in the mid-1980s had yet to be found. Apartheid had built the appearance of a natural order out of the urge to mold society and preserve a white identity. The result was, often as not, a glum resignation among those on whom it preyed.

At Crossroads—in the quiescent days before Cape Town's most renowned squatter camp burned in a vicious battle between divided blacks, some backed by the white authorities—Aletta Gwentshi watched without protest as the men of the Western Cape Administration Board (the white arbiter of black lives) tore down her shack, prying away walls and roof, as if peeling a slender onion to expose a modest core—bed and cupboard and cooking stove. Like many, she was a fugitive from the so-called homeland named the Transkei, where things—in the relativity of South Africa's miseries—were worse. Like many, she had assembled friends and relatives to build the house, and now it was being demolished. Their work done, the men from the Administration Board departed. At 4:00 P.M. they went off duty for the day. At about 4:05 P.M., Mrs. Gwentshi reassembled friends and relatives and wood and plastic to rebuild the house. And they set about their work with the same resolve as the men who had torn it down. By dusk, the shack had arisen again, waiting its next destruction.

That was the reality cloaked in the euphemism "influx control," later replaced by "orderly urbanization"—terms that denoted the urge to shield the white cities from the blacks drawn to them by the lure of jobs and betterment.

Crossroads achieved a special notoriety and became an international symbol of human uprootment. People like Mrs. Gwentshi seemed to represent a more modest metaphor for defeat and resilience. Sadly, too, the squatter camp came in time to represent a more sinister phenomenon. For years, the authorities had sought to persuade some of the squatters to move to a distant new settlement called Khayelitsha. They re-sisted, but the strains imposed by the authorities' blandishments divided them into factions. The authorities favored one group—known as the Witdoeke (meaning white cloths) because of the white head-bands they wore in combat. The Witdoeke, in turn, were opposed to the so-called comrades—the young protesters fighting the daily round of battles with the police and army in Crossroads and other Cape settle-ments such as Langa, Nyanga, and Guguletu. In 1986, the Witdoeke, with tacit official support, moved to purge Crossroads of comrades. Great swathes of the camp were burned down. Thousands of people became instant refugees and left. Some ended up where they had not wanted to go: Khayelitsha. In 1983, Cross-roads' population was estimated at 50,000. In 1988, two years after the fire and the conflict, it was esti-mated at only 30,000. The rest had become statistical monuments to "orderly urbanization."

If Crossroads was an example of where people ended up after they had circumvented official policy, then for a brief period Magopa became an equally renowned symbol of where the uprooting started. Magopa was called a black spot—the unapologetic phrase denoting a parcel of black-owned land that, with the drawing of apartheid's frontiers, had found itself caught behind the lines, encircled by white-owned land. Much official energy went into coaxing and bullying the people in such places into moving away to areas where blacks could legally reside. Apartheid's cartography did not permit black occupancy of land outside those areas designated for it—the tribal homelands; the segregated, black townships; and some squatter camps that, unlike Crossroads, were created and nurtured by the authorities. The policy produced its own arithmetic: over the quarter century ending in 1985, an academic research group sponsored in part by the South African Council of Churches estimated that 3.5 million blacks had been moved into tribal homelands and resettlement camps to tie up the loose ends of racial and ethnic separation. The ten homelands, according to recent official figures, have a registered black population of over 13 million, more than half the overall black population of 24 million.

At Magopa, near the white town of Ventersdorp in the Western Transvaal, Elisabeth Katitswe owned the Swartkop General Dealer's store where you could buy most things you might need, like blankets, and some you might not, like a bicycle bell. Her customers were the people of the Bakwena tribe, who had lived in the settlement for more than seventy years, since their forebears bought the land before the 1913 Native Trust and Land Act consigned blacks to reserves on what now amounts to just 13 percent of South Africa's surface area (the same 13 percent now covered by the tribal homelands). The fate of Mrs. Katitswe and her community came to be regarded as typical of the way those millions were moved into tribal homelands and resettlement camps.

By November 1983, the white authorities had succeeded in dividing the 500 families living at Magopa into camps for and against a move to a place called Pachsdraai, 125 miles away and close to the nominally independent homeland of Bophuthatswana, fragmented in five separate parcels of land spread over the Transvaal and the Orange Free State, and set aside for Tswana-speaking people.

Pachsdraai was set for "incorporation" into the chimera of a state represented by the homeland and recognized only by Pretoria. "Incorporation"—another euphemism—meant that, with a stroke of a pen, the land would become part of Bophuthatswana. So those who moved from Magopa to live on the dry parcel of earth at Pachsdraai would lose all claim on the citizenship of the land of their birth—South

Africa—and thus any hope of a say in its future.

Mrs. Katitswe was in the camp against the move, so she stayed on, with the others, who reckoned they formed a majority of the village. On the night of February 14, 1984, Mrs. Katitswe recalled, the security forces surrounded the place and came in with dogs and guns and bright lights and ordered the people out. The bulldozers ended what the policy had begun and the settlement ceased to exist.

Ironically enough, Mrs. Katitswe ended up in Bophuthatswana anyhow, near the small town of Bethanie where the Bakwena tribal authorities had offered them a refuge. She had brought her merchandise with her but, by late August 1985, she had been denied a license to trade. The defiance had gone, too. "It is not hard as all that, because," she said at the time, pausing for the right word, "because we are living."

After the forced removal from Magopa—and the extensive and unwelcome international publicity it engendered for Pretoria—the government announced the suspension of the policy of forced removals. Yet by late 1986 the announcement seemed hollow. Onverwacht, a huge sprawl of tin shacks in the Orange Free State, forty miles from the city of Bloemfontein and a collecting point for people of South Sotho tribal origin, had somehow swollen from 200,000 to half a million. The social engineering was continuing, an inexorable process despite the promises of change and the protests that swept the land. Later, the authorities announced that Onverwacht would be "incorporated" into the distant Quaqua—the smallest and least viable tribal homeland of them all, set aside for people speaking South Sotho—making its people citizens of a supposed nation made up of two tiny, crowded chunks of land more than a hundred miles apart, bereft of any history of nationhood or justification beyond the grand design of separation.

Such developments seemed far remote from the promises of fundamental change. All the while that President Botha was promising reform with his "new dispensation," events arranged by his own kinsmen contradicted him, as if the great unfeeling bureaucracy and the institutions of state that employed one-third of all adult Afrikaners was simply grinding on, inexorable and indifferent—unable and unwilling to change the course set by the visionaries of the Grand Apartheid or respond to the warnings of the South African leader himself. In the early 1980s, Mr. Botha had taken "Adapt or die" as his rallying cry. Apartheid's grand vision of a "white" South Africa through which blacks might only transit as "temporary sojourners," he seemed to acknowledge, had not been fulfilled, even though the bureaucracy still pursued the dream. Nine million blacks, he told his followers, had become urbanized, drawn by an economy that defeated apartheid's notion of "temporary sojourners" by demanding a permanent presence of black labor and black skills.

The 1976 uprising in Soweto had already set white leaders pondering ways of defusing the demographic time bomb. In 1979, in an effort to co-opt and control, black labor unions were legalized, only to rise, a few years later, as the very specter of black political organization that haunted white dominance.

Then, in 1983, Mr. Botha sought a mandate for what he called a new dispensation, a purported broadening of democracy to embrace nonwhite minorities—the 800,000 Indians and 2.8 million coloureds—but not the black majority. Suddenly, the amorphous sense of black disaffection found its focus. The new dispensation, with its huge implicit insult to the blacks and its effort to replace the color bar between white and nonwhite with a new distinction between black and nonblack, offered the regime's opponents the rallying point they had been awaiting.

On August 20, 1983, in a packed meeting hall in Cape Town, the UDF was formed, an umbrella movement of community and youth organizations that drew together the ideology and the figureheads of protest. Its patrons included Nelson Mandela, Bishop Tutu, and Dr. Boesak. Its co-presidents included Albertina Sisulu, wife of Walter Sisulu, jailed along with Mr. Mandela in the early 1960s. Its political ideals, many commentators noted, bore a close resemblance to those of the ANC, although it withheld formal support for the guerrilla organization's commitment to violence as the means to bring about a unitary nonracial state based on universal suffrage. Over the years of protest, the UDF, with its 600 affiliate groups, achieved primacy as the vehicle of dissent within South Africa, just as the ANC had become the externally based custodian of black protest. Both movements, with their emphasis on nonracialism, eclipsed the black consciousness groups of the 1980s that excluded white activism from the struggle. When the UDF was formed, Dr. Boesak declared, "We want all our rights . . . we want them here and we want them now." Mr. Botha had his own agenda, and he had no intention of abandoning it.

On November 2, 1983, the South African leader

went to the white voters in a referendum to seek endorsement of the new dispensation. The term implied that here was a generous offer indeed from a benevolent deity.

The Indians and the coloureds would be accorded junior roles in a segregated parliament, be able to adjudicate what were termed "own affairs"—health, schooling, and so forth—but would be subservient to the larger, white assembly in "general affairs"—defense, finance, diplomacy. With the switch from what was fancifully called "Westminster-style" democracy restricted to whites, Mr. Botha also gathered greater powers unto himself, becoming an executive State President rather than simply Prime Minister.

The dispensation made no mention of the black majority: the seeds of black democratization, the authorities argued, had already been sown in the establishment of elected black town councils in the segregated townships. The councils bore the seeds of tragedy, for they were unpopular and set blacks willing to work within the apartheid system against those who wanted to be rid of it: when violence took root, in September 1984, some of the first targets for the protesters hatred and vengeance were the black councillors living in the segregated, black town-ships, perceived by their adversaries as the stooges of the distant white administrators.

Mr. Botha interpreted the results of the referendum as a clear mandate. Two-thirds of the whites who voted had said "yes" to the changes, mixing Afrikaner and English-speaker in a new and largely urban constituency for the National Party. But the turnout represented only three-quarters of the eligible white voters (Indians and coloureds did not vote on Mr. Botha's new beneficence toward them, and when they voted for their new deputies a year later, the poll was marked by low turnouts, violence, and boycotts organized by the UDF to press its opposition to the changes). The referendum results, it could be computed, showed that half of the white population was either opposed or indifferent to Mr. Botha's dispensation, reflecting a clear trend. The very mention of departures from the canons of traditional apartheid had divided Afrikanerdom since the beginning of the decade, leading to the formation of the Conservative Party, under Dr. Treurnicht in 1982. When, in May 1987, the Conservative Party became the official opposition, it was as if the white center of gravity had lurched toward conservatism and regression, reflecting fear both of Mr. Botha's reforms and the violence that accompanied them. The division was unprecedented among the Afrikaners, unused to such uncertainty and confusion, confronting the unknown.

From a distance those small, rural towns of South Africa seemed cast in a common mold. On one side of the road would be the grain silo and the church steeple; and on the other, in Africa's winter, would be the smudge of smoke denoting the black township, a perfect, symmetrical, and fundamental division that had once seemed immutable. Behind the lace curtains and order of the white settlements, however, the new dispensation had stirred doubt and debate.

The sentiments recurred in many conversations. Mrs. Ora Terblanche, for instance, owned a guest house near Hobhouse, in the Orange Free State—the most conservative of South Africa's four provinces. In the referendum, she said, she had voted "yes"—"not because my heart told me to, my heart told me the opposite." But, she went on, "things have changed; we have to go forward, not backwards." She did not know where that route would end, and Mr. Botha sought to assure his followers that domination by the blacks (Mrs. Terblanche referred to them collectively as "these people") was not his envisaged destination.

"We do not wish to have one-man, one-vote in a unitary structure," he said the day before the referendum. "That is not what we want." He spoke for the mainstream of his people. And he did not go back on his word.

But his assurances failed to convince some and left others convinced that he was offering too little, too late to resolve the great tensions wrought by a past that had brought no peace and a future that held no easy answers. The dilemmas produced responses—among a minority of intellectual Afrikaners—that seemed to contradict the very history of their tribe.

Harald Parkendorf, the editor until 1986 of the Afrikaans evening newspaper in Johannesburg, *Die Vaderland*, offered what would once have been heresy: the future had to be posited on a notion of majority rule, and the longer hostilities continued, the less chance the whites would have to find a secure niche in that new society.

Donald Masson, a former president of the Afrikaner Institute of Commerce, seemed to come to a similar conclusion. "If we really want to lose everything," he said, "then we must hang on to everything now."

Such thoughtfulness found its counterpoint in the

roaring and thundering of Eugene Terre'Blanche, leader of the far-right Afrikaner Resistance Movement, with its swastika-like emblems and its ideology of the white state with no power-sharing or black rights.

"There is only one Volk in South Africa and that is the Afrikaner Boer," he once declared, using the Afrikaans word for farmer to frame the criterion for citizenship in his projected white state, although he is an ex-policeman himself.

Some found a home in his militarism and rhetoric and racism, his fiery speeches laden with imagery that reversed the outsider's view of things, so that the Afrikaners themselves became the oppressed and dis-possessed seeking only their rights and redemption. Mr. Terre'Blanche, at least, his friends and enemies said, had a clear vision of things—a return to an idealistic state modeled on the Boer republics of the nineteenth century run by Afrikaners for Afrikaners in defiance of blacks and British colonialism alike.

But the splintering at the fringes of Afrikanerdom left many more confused. "The man in the street is not ready for radical change," Len van Loggerenberg, an Afrikaner hotelier, said after casting a vote against Mr. Botha's limited reforms. He acknowledged that there was a problem and that South Africans had to find the solution to it themselves: South Africa, after all, was no one's colony, and no outsider could or should broker the Afrikaners' future. And neither, he said, could they simply escape. "It was easy for the guys in Rhodesia [Zimbabwe] to drop everything and run," he said. "But we cannot run away and that is why we have to find a way of living in harmony with the blacks."

"This thing," he said of Mr. Botha's constitution, "this thing is going to lead to a lot of ructions later." He was right, too, though possibly not in the way he had intended.

The new dispensation had been supposed to co-opt nonwhites and cushion whites themselves from the inevitabilities of the nation's demography. Instead, it provided the hair trigger for revolt and the fraying of the very white tribe it was supposed to redeem.

The turnaround, from Mr. Botha's triumph to the crumbling of his dreams, happened with bewilder-ing speed.

Only a year before the first emergency, President Botha had been riding a wave of self-confidence and success and had seemed almost to be leading the nation toward a kind of acceptance. On March 16, 1984, on a hot day by a sluggish stream called the Nkomati River, under a white pavilion surrounded by military tents, Mr. Botha met with the late President Samora Machel of Mozambique to sign a nonaggression treaty. "We are laying the foundation for a definitive break in the cycle of violence," President Machel said, with hopelessly misplaced optimism. A month earlier, Pretoria had reached a de facto cease-fire agreement with Angola that, like the Nkomati Agreement, was designed to undercut the guerrilla adversaries of the South African regime: the ANC, with its logistic networks and infiltration trails in Mozambique, and the South West Africa Peoples Organisation, based in Angola.

Those agreements represented the new buffers that South Africa sought to impose on its black-ruled neighbors to replace the *cordon sanitaire* once provided by white minority rule in the former Rhodesia and the Portuguese colonial rule in Angola and Mozambique.

The new deals were computed on the implicit threat that failure to cooperate would bring ruin. South Africa straddled the region's trade routes; its military forces frequently crossed borders to impose Pretoria's political will; and South Africa's strategists had no qualms about squeezing those countries that offered sanctuary to the ANC. One by one, South Africa's black-ruled neighbors—Mozambique, Angola, Swaziland, Lesotho, Zimbabwe, and Botswana—felt the weight of policies that offered a little carrot after a lot of stick. Pretoria's critics called it "destabilization."

It almost worked: in May 1984, Mr. Botha crowned his gun-barrel diplomacy with a tour of eight Western European nations that took him to the Chancellery in Bonn and Chequers, outside London. The official journey was the first of its kind by a South African leader in twenty years, and the most extensive since the National Party took power. For Mr. Botha, it must have seemed an accolade of approval, a recognition of both the ambiguous peace he had enforced on the region and of the program of modest change supposed to flourish within its iron cocoon. The strategy backfired.

On May 14, 1984—less than two months after the nonaggression treaty signed by the banks of the Nkomati River—the ANC launched a spectacular, if physically ineffective, attack on an oil refinery near Durban, as if to show that the treaty had not been the harbinger of peace that South Africa and Mozambique had predicted. In Soweto, a deeper shift seemed to have occurred. Three days after the Nkomati Agreement, some residents of the huge satellite city—home to between 1.5 and 2 million people—seemed already to have concluded that the effort to isolate blacks within the country from their champions beyond its borders had been a terrible mistake. Those sentiments seemed to foreshadow the violence to come.

"The South African government is doing what it always has—all they can to evade their responsibilities at home," said Kganyapa Molapo, a bank official. "In the same way as they blame outsiders for causing trouble, they go and try to solve the problems created by apartheid with an outside government." Reginald Ngema, a computer operator, put it more bluntly: "Talk to the people's chosen leaders. Kill and bury apartheid. It is the only solution that can bring peace to South Africa."

Emergency

This was the chronology: in September 1984, a protest over rent hikes, in Sharpeville and Sebokeng in the Vaal Triangle south of Johannesburg, turned bloody. On July 21, 1985, the violence that flowed from that conflict spurred the authorities to declare a limited State of Emergency, which came into effect at midnight. It endured until March 7, 1986. The protests continued. The Emergency, this time on a far wider scale, was reimposed on June 12, 1986, supposedly to preempt massive upheaval on June 16—the tenth anniversary of the start of the Soweto uprising.

The images, both for the participants and in the world news media, were these: tear gas billowing bright as cobalt, the flash of shotguns over the steel rims of armored vehicles, and the clanging of rocks rebounding from them; streets ablaze with barricades made of tires doused in gasoline, as if the fuel were a leitmotif that fed the revolt; the firebombs and the brutal "necklace" executions of those deemed but not necessarily proven to be collaborators.

At the center of the UDF's organizational strategy were the mass funerals when tens of thousands of blacks would gather under the banners of outlawed organizations, notably the ANC, to display grief and hone new anger in the songs of protest and the speeches that kept the flames alive, as if to reinforce the momentum so essential to what apartheid's foes wanted to achieve: the faltering, the crumbling of white resolve, the withdrawal of state power, and the acknowledgment that the official writ no longer ran at all.

That strategy produced the rallying cry that the townships should be made ungovernable, meaning that white rule, whether direct or through surrogate black councils, should be destroyed. Classes were boycotted on a wide scale to deny government educational practices that allocated much more, on a per capita basis, to white scholars in their segregated schools than to blacks in the schools allotted them. The boycotts left tens of thousands of young blacks on the streets. Black councillors and black policemen living in the townships were hounded out on pain of summary execution. The sources of official revenue—rents on the distinctive matchbox houses of the townships and income from grim beer halls owned by the authorities—were denied by rent boycotts in some places and by the torching of many a beer hall. Official control, the strategy had it, must be replaced by "people's power"—the rule of the self-appointed comrades. If discipline were to be enforced, it would be through the "people's courts," whose judgments sometimes resulted in the grisly execution of perceived collaborators in the blazing mess of a necklacing. Those killings induced a sense of horror, and official propaganda made use of them to depict black revolt as barbaric, a mindless slaughtering of black by black. But that description avoided what the comrades saw as the issue: the need to purge the black township of official control and of informers whose activities might cause the detention or even the death of protesters at the hands of the security forces. At one stage, in a township on the East Rand, Bishop Tutu himself urged a halt to the necklace executions. But his words drew little enthusiasm from his audience. "They must feel our pain," a young man said of the purported collaborators, to explain the means of their execution. Maybe outsiders were wrong to expect a uniform heroism among the foot soldiers of a harsh revolt against a harsh system.

The comrades became the nation's new warriors. Their actions sought to turn residential segregation to their own advantage: the bleak townships designed as receptacles for apartheid's "temporary sojourners" were now supposed to become the liberated areas of the revolution against the very system that created them. The presence of the police and the army was meant to ensure that they did not. In the test of wills that ensued, the comrades earned varied reputations, some for discipline and an ability to organize protest against all the odds, others for brutal measures to enforce their will.

But a common element that suffused their protest

in the miseries and poverty of the townships was a sense that their parents had failed them by submitting to apartheid's embrace instead of resisting it. If the older people were not prepared to fight, they would say, then they should move aside and leave "the struggle" to those prepared for its battles. The title "comrade" was a loose one, a form of identification among young people to establish their credentials as supporters of the UDF and the ANC, a statement of intent. It also located them in what the shadowy organizers of the protest called the "structures" of the struggle. An area, Port Elizabeth, for instance, might have its dominant figures—in this case men named Henry Fazzi and Mkuseli Jack—but, the comrades boasted, beyond them stretched a network of aides and understudies in zone and street committees able to take over in the frequent periods they spent in detention. Some have traced that form of organization to the so-called M-Plan, formulated in the 1950s by Nelson Mandela. The UDF, too, had its own unarmed regiments of "marshals"—men and women, in the Eastern Cape in particular, wearing sand-colored uniforms and black berets, who would enforce discipline at the many funerals where the speeches of leading activists offered an ideological line.

The line itself sometimes seemed amorphous since the UDF represented a coalition of many groups whose views might range from nationalism to Marxism. And the comrades, activists acknowledged, sometimes became a law unto themselves, a *lumpenproletariat* slipping beyond the control of their leaders.

Outside South Africa, some who followed the nation's torment took the government's declaration of the emergency decrees as a form of image control. But the decrees went much further, seeking to strike at the organizational heart of the protest and to shield whites from the raw visage of black rage. Thousands were detained in the assault on the "structures" of protest. Other measures, particularly the banning of mass funerals of slain activists, were designed to strike at the momentum the protest had gathered. The funerals had played a critical role since most other forms of black assembly apart from church services and soccer games had been outlawed for years. They had become the crucible of dissent, self-perpetuating rites of protest: no sooner had one group of activists been buried than another died in the clashes that followed the burial, creating more martyrs to be hymned and laid to rest in yet another funeral.

In some ways, the official strategies worked. Eventually, the momentum of the protest gave way to war-weariness. The struggle had largely been contained in the townships whose poverty and deprivation helped spawn it. The white homes, nestled behind hedges of bougainvillea in the wealthier suburbs, remained immune from direct attack.

Throughout the years of protest, millions of blacks went to work either every day or on most days in segregated white areas, in the heart of white-run cities, on white-owned farms. And, while the impression outside South Africa might have been of a daily burning of the entire nation, the reality inside its borders was different: the battles ebbed and flowed, from one point of conflagration to another. Many whites knew little of the causes of the violence or of its results. If they felt its impact, it was through anomalies in the economic interdependence of the races in which whites relied on black labor and, correspondingly, blacks depended on white wealth. Recession, predating the years of protest, had fueled black discontent, but it had also made jobs scarce; no one could afford to jeopardize them too much.

Certainly, there were strikes, huge stayaways that showed black economic muscle, highlighting the awesome demography that infused white fears on those days when no blacks arrived to run the supermarket checkouts, when the factories stalled and the maids didn't show and the dishes piled high in the kitchens. In Port Elizabeth (a city whose protesters prided themselves on being at the forefront of defiance and organization), a consumer boycott dragged on for months, forced on some black consumers, it is true, by zealous comrades, but also forcing white businessmen to do what had once been unthinkable: negotiate with leaders of black protest, such as Mr. Jack, and thereby court the anger of their own government.

When white factory owners interceded with the Afrikaner authorities to seek the release of detained black labor leaders—the very people organizing worker militancy in the factories—it seemed clear that a message had been brought home: "these people," as Ora Terblanche had called them, could not be ignored.

Demanding allies and allegiances, moreover, the protest on the streets of the townships forced the black labor movement to make a decision it had hesitated to confront. With the formation of the Confederation of South African Trade Unions (COSATU) on November 30, 1985, it cast itself as a political force in the struggle. The choice was difficult, for it risked repression that might set back for years its newly won organizational gains as a force for the economic betterment of black workers. Yet labor leaders knew they had little choice but to keep pace with the militancy of the streets. At its inaugural rally in December 1985, COSATU—the biggest black labor federation in South Africa's history—came into being with a flourish of political demands for disinvestment by Western corporations, the withdrawal of troops from the townships, and the scrapping of the pass laws. Its very name evoked the 1950s Congress Alliance of anti-apartheid movements, and its leaders soon traveled to Harare and met with their counterparts in the ANC.

Yet the economy survived strikes, sanctions, and disinvestment. Much more worrisome was the calling of part of the foreign debt by Western, mainly American, banks. That led to the collapse of the currency, the rand, and cast doubt on the ability of Pretoria, suddenly a net exporter of capital, both to pay its foreign debt and to finance what was left of its reform policies at home.

Literally translated, the word *apartheid* means apartness or separateness. The years of protest seemed to highlight how efficiently the apartheid system had worked: more than ever, South Africa was a land composed of two competing realities, divided by race, official policy, and urban planning designed to achieve more than just physical separation. The years of violence seemed to deepen the gulf, confirming the prejudices and prejudgments of both sides.

"We don't know what happens over there," a white Rotarian in Uitenhage said one day in April 1985. "Over there" was the black township of Kwa-Nobuhle, where eight black protesters were being buried. "They go their way and we go ours," he said, and continued his barbecue of fat sausage over charcoal. Only a few weeks earlier, police had shot and killed nineteen blacks marching with thousands of others from Langa, a township on the other side of Uitenhage, to KwaNobuhle. Their march, apparently, had gotten too close to a white suburb.

With the exception of civil rights groups that prided themselves on nonracialism, the contact points between the races were few. Workplaces such as mines and factories provided some, framed by the distinction between boss and worker. The white home was probably another, as much as could be permitted by the ties that bind maid and "madam." The conflict itself offered a third, sad alternative: a generation of the nation's youth—white conscripts and black protesters—made contact from opposite ends of a gun barrel.

For months on end, the townships refused to be

quiet, challenging the authorities to contain them, to deploy the white conscripts and the regular police, to create front forces of ill-trained black policemen in the effort to halt the struggle whose images in the distant West invited sanctions and disinvestment and deepening isolation. In military terms, it was an uneven battle.

Only rarely did the guns of the ANC reach the unarmed protesters of the townships, reinforcing an assessment among activists and intellectuals that if power were to be taken, it would be seized from within, albeit in the name of the ANC and its leaders, but not by some liberating army sent from beyond South Africa's borders to challenge Pretoria's armed might. The assessment reflected some of the ambiguities surrounding the oldest of South Africa's black resistance movements, whose history dates to the formation of its forerunner, the South African Native National Congress, in 1912.

The ANC's black, gold, and green banner had become a rallying point of dissent, legitimized in black eyes—like the red flag of its ally, the South African Communist Party (SACP)—by the authorities' very revulsion at their twin message of liberation and revolution.

The relationship between the ANC and the SACP is complex and shrouded in deliberate secrecy. While some SACP leaders sit on the central committee of the ANC, the two organizations have sought to maintain distinct identities, the ANC as the nationalist front that sees its task as "liberation," the SACP, orthodox and pro-Soviet in its international relations, as a vanguard Marxist party seeking a workers' state. Between them, with their jointly sponsored guerrilla campaign, they had kept alive a hope among many blacks that, some day, it would be different, that someone at least was fighting on their behalf. Yet when the protest of the mid-1980s erupted, neither organization could honestly claim to have orchestrated the stirrings of revolt.

Months before the ANC made its call for the townships to be made ungovernable, for instance, some black settlements had been far beyond the reach of official control, forcing the distant, exiled leaders in Lusaka to formulate a strategy reflecting the new realities that had already emerged inside the country. A new youthful constituency, zealous and unarmed, with no interest in compromise or patient strategy, had arisen, fighting in the ANC's name—not at its initial command.

Free Nelson Mandela, the comrades chanted, though most had not been born when he and seven other leaders of the ANC were sentenced to life imprisonment on terrorism and sabotage charges in 1964. Let Tambo return, they said. Go well, Spear of the Nation, they sang to the ANC's guerrillas in one of the most haunting of the refrains they called freedom songs.

The roots of the ANC's support were spread wide across the country, partly by default since the authorities' actions against dissent had left no other vehicle for black aspirations, no channel for lawful political organization by the black majority. Partly, too, the organization drew on a respectability and legitimacy derived from decades of protest that had embraced many generations and ideological shadings. It had led peaceful protest against the pass laws in the 1950s. In 1955, the ANC had embraced its manifesto, "The Freedom Charter"—a document that began from the premise that "South Africa belongs to all who live in it, black and white." The organization promised democracy and equality, and a redistribution of land and wealth—promises that the white authorities interpreted as a blueprint for massive nationalization and Marxist rule. Its leaders, including Nelson Mandela, had faced the protracted Treason Trial from 1956 to 1961. Only after the Sharpeville killings of sixty-nine blacks by the police in 1960 and the subsequent banning of the ANC and other protest movements did

the organization formally embrace "armed struggle." The first attacks by the ANC's newly formed military wing, Umkhonto we Sizwe (Spear of the Nation), under its commander Nelson Mandela, took place in December 1961 with bombings of official buildings in Durban, Johannesburg, and Port Elizabeth. By August 1962, Mandela had again been arrested; he has not known freedom since. But the sabotage campaign of the 1960s and the guerrilla war that has continued since then also help explain the ANC's support: though often botched and ineffective, guerrilla attacks—supposedly directed primarily at economic and military targets rather than civilian "soft" targets—sought to demonstrate that the white state was not so omnipotent as the burden of apartheid on black shoulders seemed designed to prove.

There was an additional, paradoxical factor: Pretoria's own obsession with infiltrating and breaking ANC had imparted a legitimacy and glamor. Officials at once denigrated ANC as disorganized and ineffective, yet sought support for their crusade against it by calculating that it had caused $500 million worth of damage in sabotage acts between 1960 and 1984.

The ANC was, by official accounts, at once there and not there. Rarely did the guerrillas have more than a few dozen of their numbers inside South Africa at any one time, and yet they represented, by official accounts, the cutting edge of a "total onslaught" orchestrated by Moscow against South Africa. Supposedly bereft of infrastructure and support, the guerrillas nonetheless managed to slip by South Africa's security services, which thought of themselves as being among the most pervasive and efficient in the world. The results were sometimes more ambiguous, playing into the enemy's hand instead of denting its resolve. In May 1983, a car bomb outside air force headquarters in Pretoria killed nineteen people, many of them black civilians who happened to be passing by at the time. That hardly seemed commensurate with the aims of an organization that championed the cause of the same people as had just died on the streets of the capital. When, at a news conference in Nairobi, he took responsibility for the explosion, Oliver Tambo seemed shaken by the results of the attack. But the damage had been done, and, as the protest inside South Africa continued, the ANC itself formally acknowledged that the distinction between "hard" economic and military targets and "soft" civilian targets was bound to blur. The realities bore out the assessment: in December 1985, an ANC guerrilla said

to be acting independently of official orders planted a bomb in a shopping mall frequented by white vacationers near Durban. Five whites died as a result.

In early 1985, the organization seemed taken by surprise, unable to harness the great ground swell of revolt that had come from within.

The new dispensation offered the black majority the choice between co-option into Mr. Botha's projected changes and revolt against them. There was no middle ground. Many townships chose revolt. The official response was the repression of what, to the authorities, seemed a violent challenge on their very existence.

South Africa's first Emergency came into effect the day after a huge funeral in honor of the murdered activist Matthew Goniwe and three of his colleagues in the small Eastern Cape town of Cradock. The Emergency decree, declared in thirty-six districts under the Public Safety Act, gave the authorities wide powers of search and detention without trial and the right to withhold the identity of those detained. Detainees had no legal rights to see lawyers or visitors. Many of those detained complained of torture by electric shock and innovative brutalities, such as the "helicopter"—suspending a captive from a pole and then spinning the person around. That official behavior seemed, in some ways, to match the bitterness of repression on the streets, where the security forces disposed weapons that ranged from sjambok whips to automatic rifles to confront the cruder weapons of their adversaries. Press coverage of protest was severely restricted by the 1985 decree, although not nearly so comprehensively as under the subsequent nationwide Emergency that came into force in 1986. Police and army officers were indemnified against legal actions relating to their enforcement of the decree. The coincidence of the declaration with Mr. Goniwe's funeral was not inappropriate.

On the day of his burial, the sense of looming confrontation seemed almost tangible. In the dust of the township, amid the songs urging violent revolt, giant banners were unfurled—those of the ANC, and the hammer and sickle of the Soviet Union—a great taunt to the authorities with their armored cars and police reinforcements massed on the hill overlooking the township, and on the scrubby, flat field just beyond the graveyard where the four men would be buried under markers painted in the ANC colors. (The songs became a leading feature of such sad events, invariably lionizing the ANC's guerrillas, accompanied by foot-stomping dances that mimicked guerrillas in action, firing from the hip with imaginary AK-47 assault rifles.)

Presumably, the police and army commanders in Cradock knew that the Emergency announcement would be made that day and that those very banners of revolt would be used to explain the need for stern measures against the "total onslaught" when film of them was broadcast on state television that night. It was a marked departure from the official practice of keeping such images away from the nation's viewers.

Clergymen, always at the forefront of the protest in one way or another, were caught on film, framed against the snapping pennants of Soviet communism, a propaganda coup for the authorities that was, in reality, a reflection of the breadth of the coalition they faced: from nationalist church leaders to avowed communists.

The clenched fists punched incessantly at the air. For months, the protest had rolled from township to township, gathering momentum, at once capricious and inexorable, easing in one place only to flare in another. Cradock itself had exemplified the manner in which protest over local issues—the sacking of Mr.

Goniwe, the headmaster, proposed rent hikes—became magnified and blurred with the overriding issue of apartheid facing the nation.

For months, the latest uprising had been pushing at the gates of apartheid's citadel, demanding satisfaction, change, liberation, and revolution. The uprising had developed like Africa's rains, in those hot days when the clouds form and bruise the sky but do not break and yield only more heat and tension and no rain, for days on end, until the deluge comes.

Apartheid must go. Free Nelson Mandela. The messengers of rage battering at the Afrikaner door: surrender power to the people.

Something had to give, and what gave was the last pretense of hope for a political exodus from the crisis, for a widened acceptance of Mr. Botha's proposed reforms by the black majority. The Emergency made the formal declaration of a war that had already started.

"I am not prepared to lead white South Africans and other minority groups on a road to abdication and suicide," Mr. Botha said, three weeks after the first Emergency was declared, in a major speech that offered a bellicose response to the mounting foreign and domestic pressure for fundamental change.

"Listen, my friends, listen," Mr. Botha said. "Destroy white South Africa and our influence in this subcontinent of southern Africa, and this country will drift into factions, strife, chaos, and poverty."

"We have never given in to outside demands and we are not going to do so. South Africa's problems will be solved by South Africans and not by foreigners. We are not going to be deterred from what we think best," he said, "nor will we be forced into a position of doing what we don't want to do."

South Africa, Mr. Botha said, was crossing the Rubicon.

"There can be no turning back. We now have a manifesto for the future of our country, and we must embark on a program of positive action in the months and years that lie ahead."

That manifesto, framed by white planners to redefine the mechanisms of white exclusivism and supremacy, nonetheless departed profoundly from the notions of domination encased in Hendrik Verwoerd's apartheid, since it acknowledged a position for nonwhites, however subordinate, in the ruling of the land.

There would, Mr. Botha promised, be a place for urban blacks in some kind of undefined political structures, some form of South African citizenship for blacks outside the homelands, and "co-responsibility and participation" in a new, multiracial future.

Yet the offer of partnership was flawed from the start because, Mr. Botha seemed to say, he would deal only with those blacks who had been co-opted into the system, not with those the majority patently wanted: Nelson Mandela and Oliver Tambo.

And any new order would be based on the notion that South Africa was a land of minorities, in which each minority was entitled to "self-determination," the code word for white domination. Not one single black leader of any stature endorsed the plan.

Mr. Botha's mood that night in Durban, hectoring the entire outside world, wagging his forefinger like an irate headmaster, was so belligerent that even the most charitably disposed outsiders found it difficult to sympathize with him, caught between a uncontrollable protest demanding his abdication and a white constituency whose opposition to any appeasement seemed to grow daily.

Mr. Botha could not satisfy both and did not wish to. The speech, tipped in advance by some newspapers and government leaders in the West as a platform for the announcement of huge reforms that he had never envisaged, restated his position—commitment to the twin promises of repression of those who dissented and small rewards for those who crossed the lines to support the modest changes he proposed.

South Africans, he said, "will not accept the principle of one-man, one-vote in a unitary system. Such an arrangement would lead to domination of one over the others and it would lead to chaos. Consequently, I reject it as a solution."

And that was that. The Rubicon had, indeed, been crossed, in ways Mr. Botha had not intended.

The protest was not stemmed. The political "dispensation" had been rejected by those it was supposed to embrace. More significant than the rock-throwing and the barricades, the revolt seemed to move into a more advanced stage. "These people" started creating alternatives, street committees, zone committees that could enforce a consumer boycott or get protesters onto the streets to try to fill the vacuum created by the breakdown of official control—not everywhere, but in many parts of the Eastern Cape and in the townships east and west of Johannesburg on the gold-bearing Rand. There was talk, too, of alternative education, classes in which blacks would be taught that their history and dreams should not be framed by reference to arrival of Jan van Riebeck in the Cape in

1652. In some parts, on a small scale, there seemed also to be cautious venturing across the color lines that Mr. Botha did not wish to countenance.

In the Eastern Cape, Molly Blackburn, a white liberal activist from Port Elizabeth who died in a car crash just after Christmas in 1985, had chronicled official repression of the black townships and was welcomed in them in a way that transcended South Africa's racial stereotypes. There were some in South Africa's white liberal establishment who thought Mrs. Blackburn naive, duped by unscrupulous black revolutionaries. But when she was buried on January 2, 1986, more than 10,000 black civilians streamed into Port Elizabeth to mourn her, ordinary people of all ages who did not seem to have been enlisted by some nefarious plot. Black nationalist chants and Christian hymns accompanied the service, the biggest in recent history for a white campaigner against apartheid. "Africans in this country," said Mkuseli Jack, "are walking tall in the trail she blazed."

In a string of small towns in the Eastern Cape and in Port Elizabeth, boycotts of white-owned stores by black consumers forced whites to negotiate with the blacks on a basis that acknowledged mutual dependence. In a way, such moments represented no more than a suspension of hostilities, interludes in a conflict sustained by racial distinction: many of the blacks who participated in such negotiations were detained by the white authorities.

In Natal province, Chief Buthelezi's movement negotiated a blueprint for power-sharing with whites, a plan that suggested provincial leadership by a black figure whose actions would be limited by white minority guarantees, granting them the power of veto. The plan, despite being lauded by some whites who feared the ANC as far too radical, gathered no pace, rejected by the UDF and the ANC because it fell short of a straight system of one-man, one vote, and ignored by Pretoria because it went too far toward it.

The ANC had long called the Zulu leader a stooge because he had opted to become chief minister of the KwaZulu tribal homeland and therefore was depicted as collaborating with the system of apartheid. In response, the Chief pointed out that he had refused Pretoria's offer of nominal independence for Kwa-Zulu, thereby ensuring that 6 million Zulus were not erased from the apartheid arithmetic that determined who might claim South African citizenship.

The rivalry extended to questions of turf and status and dispute over the role of "armed struggle," which the ANC advocates and Inkatha formally rejects.

Frequently the tensions among people of color in Natal province, where Zululand in located, spilled into bloodletting. In August 1985, Zulus and Indians had fought each other in battles that seemed rooted locally in black resentments of the Indians who predominate there, but the battles tapped into the tensions between Inkatha and the UDF.

The brief and bloodstained race war brought Chief Buthelezi's Inkatha *impis*, the traditional word for battalions, onto the streets in force, supposedly to police the black townships. The authorities seemed to make no attempt to halt them, suggesting a tolerance that would not be extended to their rivals.

When Durban's battles were over, scores lay dead and the fighting had left its own particular monument: the erstwhile home of Mohandas K. Gandhi lay pillaged and burned. The museum containing his memorabilia had been looted. It had been built as a shrine to nonviolent protest. The years of protest, however, witnessed the withering of such faint hopes for a peaceful outcome to the nation's turmoil.

At Molly Blackburn's funeral, Dr. Boesak, president of the World Alliance of Reformed Churches, spoke of the great potential many sense South Africa should have. "Molly continues in death what she did in life," he declared. "She brings us together in anticipation of what this country of ours could and should be."

But those hopes had their counterpoint. Outside the church, the comrades sang a lilting song whose words belied its gentle tones. "There is no freedom in South Africa without bloodshed. There is no freedom in South Africa without war."

Choices

In December 1986, Archbishop Desmond Tutu had just returned from a trip abroad and was at a Johannesburg's Jan Smuts airport awaiting a flight to Cape Town where his official residence, Bishopscourt, is located in the otherwise white part of the city.

Two flights were boarding at the time—one for Cape Town, one for Port Elizabeth—and about 400 people checked through to the lounge.

The Archbishop was the only one of those people submitted to the indignity of a body search. As was his wont, he made some kind of joke about it, but there was a bitter edge to his self-deprecating laugh: where else, after all, would the police suspect an Archbishop—the leader of the country's Anglicans, black and white, and a Nobel Peace Prize winner—of toting a gun under his cassock? Where else would they select an Archbishop for a body search?

The point was simply to remind the Archbishop of where he came from, of who and what he was as far as the police were concerned: just another black man in South Africa. As he often points out, he does not need too many reminders.

There he is, an Archbishop, in his fifties, the leader of his flock. Yet he has no passport, only a travel document that lists his citizenship as "undeterminable at present," and, in a land that gives the franchise to whites from the age of eighteen upward, he is not allowed a vote to determine his country's future. Where else can that happen?

The protests confronted the Archbishop, as they did many others, with agonizing choices. To maintain credibility among the black majority within the black communities he served, he needed to pay homage to their zeal; as a man of religion, he needed to discourage the protest violence without condoning the violence perpetrated by others.

Yet the authorities labeled the Archbishop a high priest of violence. Many whites took the official word at face value and scorned him for it. But the perspective from the townships was different: at Duduza township on the East Rand, he and Bishop Simeon Nkoane rescued a man identified as an informer who was about to be necklaced. When he spoke out against the practice, it was at the risk of being labeled irrelevant to the course his community was charting. The hazards were equivalent when he met, as he occasionally did, with President Botha, winning no concessions yet pursuing peace as a moderate, with authorities all too ready to depict him as an extremist.

The Archbishop agonized over his calls for sanctions and disinvestment, but, in the end, it must have seemed the only option to violence.

And neither could he distance himself from the struggle that took many forms: after the final crackdown on the UDF, of which he was a patron, and on sixteen other anti-apartheid groups on February 24 and 25, 1988, the voices of the church were the only ones left unsilenced.

Others made their choices, too, like Winnie Mandela, who broke the various bans and restrictions on her movements in order to be arrested for returning from Brandfort to her home in Soweto in December 1985. Like others, she could not remain silent while the land burned with protest, and her actions, though criticized by some in the struggle for their flamboyance, nonetheless represented a calculated act of disobedience, designed to bring further opprobrium on the regime.

But of all the dilemmas confronted by black South Africans, the most harrowing seemed to fall on people who had not won fame or prominence, had not garnered the slender protection of celebrity, or even really fallen foul of the authorities in any dramatic way.

The struggle did not just involve the big-name players, or the highly politicized comrades, but it also involved a great mass of people caught up in impossible choices.

Consider, for instance, Nyameka Goniwe. After her husband's murder, the funeral that was to offer such a momentous turning point in the struggle loomed not only as a question of politics, but also as questions demanding a more immediate solution: how would the family mourners be fed when the nearby white stores were being boycotted in protest at the murder? What about water and rest rooms and loudspeakers for the day? And worst of all, what would she do with Nyaniso, her three-year-old son?

In 1977, Mrs. Goniwe said, she had attended the funeral of Steve Biko and had been troubled by the wailing of children at the burial of the Black Consciousness leader who had died in police custody. Now she would have to make a decision herself: to shelter Nyaniso or expose him to the harshness of the land and strife to which he was one small heir.

Or consider Mrs. Victoria Gasela, who lived in Alexandra township, outside Johannesburg. If ever one person seemed to symbolize the extremes of impossible choices open to the black majority, it was she. Her husband was a black policeman. Her daughter Mathilda—one of nine children—was a local political activist. Because of her husband's position, the comrades had tried to burn down her home. Because of her daughter's activities, the young woman, aged twenty-six, had been detained under the Emergency decree of 1985.

"When your child is arrested," Mrs. Gasela said, "it is like death."

And when your husband is a policeman prey to the wrath of the comrades, "you just live like birds—there is no sleep."

The myriad small pains added up to something larger, a realization that while the guns, the armor, the money, and the resources were in the hands of the country's rulers, South Africa had nonetheless been shaken to its roots.

The authorities had been forced to acknowledge implicitly in their Emergency decrees that they could secure their tenure only by coercion. That in itself displayed the limits of white power, for it showed theirs to be a power without roots of broad consent, never resting easily with itself or with the people on whom it preyed.

White self-confidence had been dented. The emigration figures, mainly among English-speaking whites, increased rapidly. The Afrikaner strategies of change—the government's limited reforms, embracing nonwhites but denying the black majority—had been denied by the same majority that they so pointedly excluded from power.

Far from South Africa's shores, in response to the images of rage and fire, sanctions and disinvestment—however flawed and ambiguous—had become a reality.

And worst of all for the self-image of South Africa's government and business elite, the country had been forced to reschedule its foreign debt, just like a Third-World problem child, contradicting the cherished notion that South Africa, by virtue of the distant roots of its rulers, belonged to a civilized Western and Christian community of nations.

And all those shifts and tremors had been set off by rocks and gasoline bombs arrayed against a continent's most powerful security forces. Such change could not have come without the imparting of knowledge to all: for whites a glimpse of vulnerability, their Achilles heel laid bare, and for blacks a sense, an inkling of a new ability to force change.

From 1984 to 1987 the battle left no clear victors. Afrikaner will—the collective nerve of 2.8 million whites thousands of miles and many centuries away from their European kinsmen—had reasserted itself, and continued to reassert itself into 1988 when, finally, the activities of the UDF and the few remaining resistance organizations still operating openly were formally restricted.

Those who had pontificated, far from South Africa, that a revolution had entered its decisive phase were proved wrong, largely because they had underestimated the determination and the ability of the Afrikaner minority to hang on to its dominance.

Why, indeed, should Afrikaners surrender, as the outsiders demanded of them, when they had patently and visibly not lost. Why should they, by their analysis of things, permit themselves to be swamped in the same tidal wave of majority rule that had so obviously brought tyranny and decay to much of the continent north of them?

And so, Afrikaners persisted in the belief that with force and dominance, they might yet mold a solution, even though their policies had been proven bankrupt.

The other side understood, too, that what had brought the successes of those years when at least 2,500 died was not only the rocks and the firebombs, the barricades, and the sacrifice. With unprecedented doggedness, black will had also asserted itself. What was really important was the organization—sometimes rooted in coercion—that marshaled black numerical strength behind an identifiable stated cause and maintained a momentum that took years to break. Denied a place in the national political forum, black activists had established their own, in organizations like the UDF and the labor federation COSATU, both closely linked to the ANC. The alliance offered no comfort to white privilege.

What the successive Emergencies attacked was not a mob throwing rocks but the organization that stood behind the crowd, the "structures" that kept the faith alive in the onslaught against the authorities, the sense of impending victory that kept the anger boiling— one more push, comrades, and the citadel will fall.

The government called it a "revolutionary climate." And that is what it sometimes seemed to be.

When the mood began to dissipate, as the weariness of attrition set in, the Afrikaners could breathe again. Yet still there were many who argued that the war was by no means over, that the tactics of organized resistance had been honed and would not simply be forgotten.

"The state can still tear apart the body of organised political activity," Tom Lodge of Johannesburg's Witwatersrand University, the author of a major work on black politics in South Africa, wrote in late 1987 in the left-wing publication *Work in Progress*. "What is questionable though is whether the psychological effects of doing so will be as durable as was the case after the state's clamp-down at the beginning of the 1960s.

"The culture of black radicalism," he said, "may be much more resilient this time."

—Alan Cowell
Athens, April 1988

Author's note: I was able to report on the characters and incidents portrayed in this essay as a result of an assignment as the Johannesburg Bureau Chief of the *New York Times* from 1983 to early 1987. I am thankful to the editors of the *New York Times* for according me this privilege. The conclusions drawn in the essay are my own.

PAGES 56 AND 57: *Contestants prepare for a beauty pageant at a country fair in the northern border town of Messina.*

*Minister of Foreign Affairs Roelof "Pik" Botha
dancing at a party in his honor in East London on the
campaign trail preceding the all-white 1987 general
elections.*

Students take a break in the shade during cricket practice at the Diocesan College, called Bishops, an exclusive boys' high school in Cape Town.

PAGES 60 AND 61: *Town officials of Boksburg, one of the string of mining and industrial towns east of Johannesburg, stand to attention with dignitaries from surrounding municipalities at a ceremony awarding State President Pieter W. Botha the key to the city.*

The Dutch Reformed Church is the dominant religious order for Afrikaners; its Calvinism pervades Afrikaner culture. In Swartruggens, a rural farming area in the Western Transvaal, deacons drawn from the congregation read from the Bible at a Sunday Service.

PAGE 64: *Daniel Brits with his seven-year-old daughter Susan in Montclair, a suburb of subsidized government housing northwest of Johannesburg.*

PAGE 65: *Dannie and Tienie Nortje, farmers outside Swartruggens, with their wedding photograph taken some thirty years ago. Nortje's family trekked by oxwagon from the Cape and settled on their farm in 1903.*

PAGES 66 AND 67: *A high school student waits for the train in a suburban Cape Town railroad station; two women employed as domestic workers in the white suburbs walk past to the nonwhite end of the platform.*

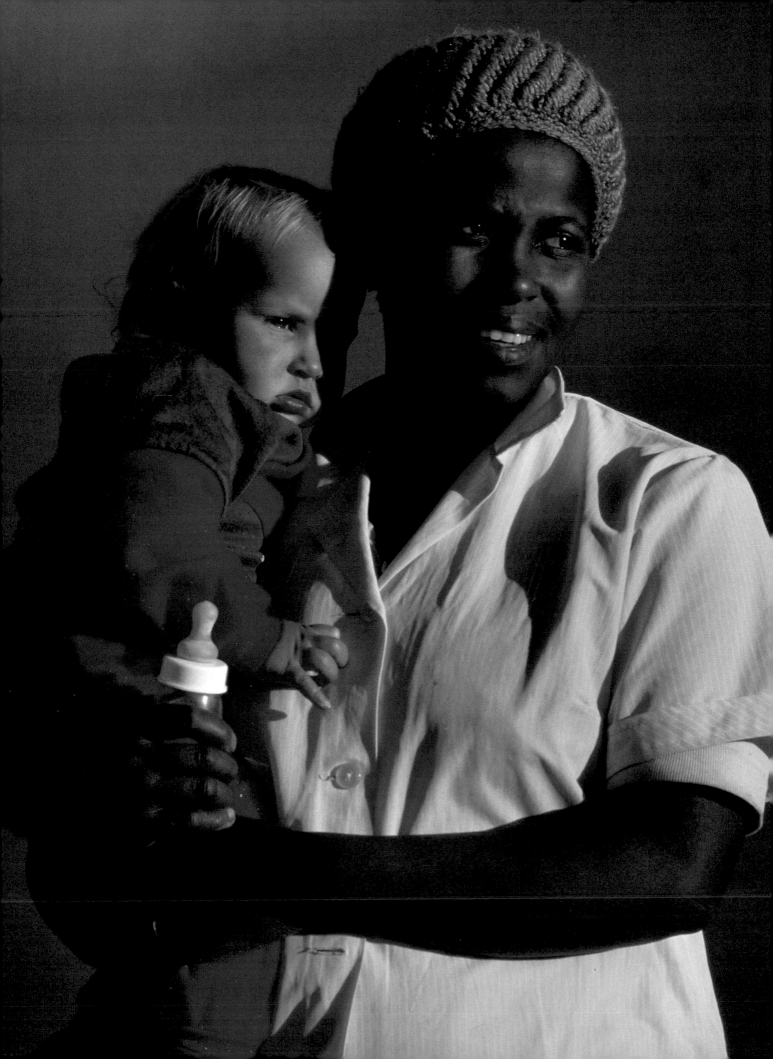

A meter man empties a parking meter in Bethlehem in
the Orange Free State while his black assistant stands
ready to carry the coins.

FACING PAGE: *Paulina Putlani and her charge
Nicholas Olivier in Hobhouse, a rural village in the
predominantly Afrikaans-speaking Orange Free State.*

Johan Richter, an Orange Free State farmer, and one of his laborers, William Gathie, in the farmer's bakkie, *or pickup truck.*

PAGES 72 AND 73: *Johan Richter makes a telephone call in his bedroom while a fourteen-year-old domestic servant brushes the carpet.*

PAGES 74 AND 75: *The pharmacy in Bedford, a farming village in the Eastern Cape.*

PAGES 76 AND 77: *Theuns and Johanna Van Staden say grace in their home outside Groot Marico in the Western Transvaal while their domestic servant, Sanna Kidige, stands by to help serve lunch.*

PAGES 78 AND 79: *Billy Van Der Merwe, a prominent Afrikaner lawyer, lunches with his partners in their Johannesburg office.*

*Unseated during a polocross game outside Messina in
the Northern Transvaal, a local farmer's son angrily
stalks away from his horse.*

A boy plays golf in an open field outside Alexandra township, which abuts Johannesburg's affluent northern suburbs.

PAGES 82 AND 83: *A Xhosa woman in the mountains of the Transkei. This tribal homeland became "independent" in 1976, thus depriving its residents of South African citizenship.*

PAGES 84 AND 85: *Late afternoon in Soweto.*

Archbishop Desmond Tutu with young parishioners at a Soweto church where he had just given communion. The archbishop, who heads South Africa's Anglican church, is abhorred by conservatives because of his support of sanctions and diplomatic isolation.

PAGE 88: *Young women stroll through New Brighton, one of the oldest—and most politically defiant—townships in the Eastern Cape. At one point during the Emergency, police fenced off the entire township with barbed wire, leaving only one entrance.*

PAGE 89: *A farmworker and his daughter play guitar. The family are laborers on the Orange Free State farm of Johan Richter.*

*Children play "Simon Says" in their corrugated iron
schoolroom in Crossroads, a squatter settlement outside
Cape Town. During the unrest that began in 1984,
the government-funded black school system virtually
ground to a halt because of widespread boycotts.*

The classroom of an Afrikaans-language elementary school in the Orange Free State town of Ficksburg.

PAGES 92 AND 93: *A farm laborer's daughter stands at the doorway of the family home on a farm near Welkom.*

PAGES 94 AND 95: *Residents of Tembisa, a black township in an industrial area between Johannesburg and Pretoria, relax outside the front doors of their one-bedroom houses.*

PAGES 96 AND 97: *Two Soweto women walking from a Sunday morning church service.*

PAGES 98 AND 99: *In Johannesburg commuter trains, black train conductors may be assigned to the first-class white sections.*

PAGES 100 AND 101: *A Zulu woman and her two children ride home to their village south of Durban in a railroad car reserved for nonwhites.*

In June 1986, black vigilantes routed many residents of Crossroads, a squatter camp outside Cape Town, destroying homes and buildings, including the Empilisweni clinic. One of few medical facilities for a community exceeding 30,000, the clinic has since been rebuilt.

PAGES 104 AND 105: *Soweto graffiti. The words are the title of Alan Paton's famous novel about a Zulu priest's search for his fugitive son in the harsh townships of Johannesburg.*

PAGES 106 AND 107: *Residents of Alexandra township outside Johannesburg return home following a mass funeral for unrest victims.*

PAGES 108 AND 109: *Morning beverage in hand, a resident of Port Elizabeth's New Brighton township talks with neighbors from the window of her home.*

PAGES 110 AND 111: *Children at play in the unpaved streets of Soweto.*

Reverend Nico Smith and his wife Ellen moved to Mamelodi township, outside Pretoria, in 1984 shortly after the minister, formerly a conservative Afrikaner and a member of the secret Broederbond Afrikaner organization, accepted an invitation to preach to this all-black congregation. Explaining his very unusual move, Smith said he wanted to live among the people he served instead of leaving every day for a "comfortable white suburb."

FACING PAGE: *Troop patrols and the armored vehicle known as a Casspir have become a daily feature of life in South Africa's black townships.*

PAGE 114: *A farm laborer's child on her way home from the local grocery store outside Bloemfontein in the Orange Free State.*

PAGE 115: *The reference book, or pass—one of South Africa's most infamous symbols of black subjugation—was abolished in 1986 and replaced with an identity document. Critics contend the new system has simply replaced one form of control with another; blacks are not entitled to the new card unless they can prove they were permanent residents of "white" South Africa before June 1986. This effectively excludes residents of "independent" homelands, relegating them to a life of rural poverty.*

PAGES 116 AND 117: *Mother and child stand in front of their home on an Orange Free State farm, where the family members are employed as laborers. Farm and domestic workers are excluded from laws prescribing basic work conditions such as hours and sick leave, and can earn as little as eighty-five cents a day.*

Jan Naude speaks to a laborer on his Henneman farm in the predominantly Afrikaans-speaking Orange Free State. The province, one of the old Boer republics, is considered South Africa's most conservative.

Johan Richter gives instructions to a young gardener on the family farm outside Bloemfontein. It is quite common for children to work as farm laborers for very low wages.

A worker sorts potatoes on the Naude farm.

On Sunday, their only day off, women dance outside their home on a farm in Welkom.

Pages 122 and 123: *Cilliers Naude, his girlfriend, and his niece relax on the Naude farm outside Henneman. The women in the background, who are farm laborers, are fetching water for their homes.*

Two Free State farmers supervising the corn harvest drink a refreshment brought by two domestic servants, who wait to take back the bottle.

A young woman stands at the doorway of her one-room home on the Jan Naude family farm outside Welkom.

FACING PAGE: *The woman bathes herself in a washbasin; few farm workers have running water in their homes.*

PAGES 128 AND 129: *Farm workers at home on a Free State farm. The husband works a sixty-hour week for a monthly wage of about thirty dollars and a ration of cornmeal. The wife is employed as a domestic servant. According to researchers, women employed on farms generally earn half as much as men.*

PAGES 130 AND 131: *Dancing in a Transkei village.*

PAGES 132 AND 133: *Shepherds tend their herds outside Ugie on the Transkei border at the foot of the Drakensberg mountains.*

Two white youths paddle down the Vaal River in Virginia in the Orange Free State, past a black church service on the riverbank. Such outdoor services are common in the black community, particularly among indigenous black Christian sects.

Lawn bowls at an all-white club outside Durban. The man helping pick up the woods—as the balls are called—receives small tips for his services.

Piet Pretorius, a gold miner, eats lunch while
watching a Sunday afternoon cricket game in his home
near the Kinross Gold Mine, about sixty miles east of
Johannesburg.

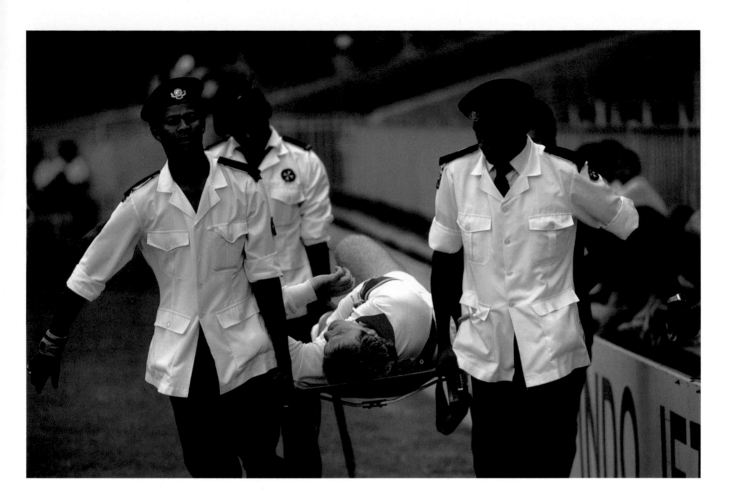

Medics carry an injured rugby player off the field during a Currie Cup game at Newlands in Cape Town. Since sporting boycotts excluded South Africa from international events, national tournaments like the Currie Cup have assumed great importance.

Tienie Nortje burns the feathers off a chicken she has just slaughtered while her husband Dannie watches.

FACING PAGE: *Reena Naude, wife of an Orange Free State farmer, takes a telephone call under the mounted heads of buck her husband shot.*

*A backyard barbecue in Claremont, a poor
Johannesburg suburb.*

At a church social in Henneman, butchered pigs are
sold to raise money.

143

Students at Stellenbosch University, the country's most
venerable Afrikaans-language college, drink beer at
the Die Akker Pub on campus. A small but significant
number of students at the university, alma mater of
many prominent government figures, have recently
shaken the Afrikaner establishment by questioning state
policy.

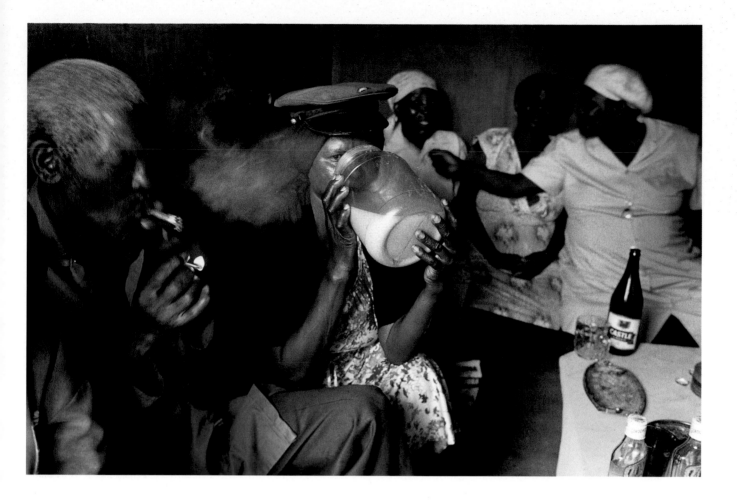

Township residents drink home-brewed beer at a shebeen—or speakeasy—outside Durban.

PAGES 146 AND 147: *In their one-room home in the black township outside Lambert's Bay, Jeff Venter kisses his seven-month-old daughter Melissa as his wife Lillie rests. Although laws outlawing mixed-race marriages were rescinded in 1985, the Venters say it has been almost impossible to find a community where they are accepted.*

PAGES 148 AND 149: *President P. W. Botha chats with the wife of the white administrator of Natal province at the launching of the KwaZulu-Natal Joint Executive Authority in November 1987. The multiracial authority, which has no legislative powers, will coordinate administration of the province and KwaZulu, a populous tribal homeland scattered in eight pieces around Natal. KwaZulu's powerful chief minister, Mangosuthu Gatsha Buthelezi, also on stage with his wife, is reviled by many black leaders for his willingness to deal with the state.*

Hannes Myburgh, whose family owns Meerlust, the oldest vineyard in the country, attends the funeral of one of his laborers.

PAGES 152 AND 153: *Gold miners wait for an elevator after working an all-night shift in a mine outside Welkom. Most black miners are migrant workers housed on mine compounds in single-sex hostels. They see their families once a year.*

Gold miner Piet Pretorius returns from his shift. He
has used the ground-level elevator; the black miners
are transported separately. In September 1986, a fire
in this shaft of the Kinross Gold Mine killed 177
miners, 5 of them white and 172 black.

More than one mile underground, Piet Pretorius and
a black laborer drill into the rock to place explosives.
Pretorius is in charge of a hundred black workers at
Kinross; officials with the black National Union of
Mineworkers calculate that a white miner earns at
least three times more than a black.

PAGES 156 AND 157: A miner, shift complete,
relaxes in the locker room at Kinross.

BOTH: *Johannes Shozi and his "city" wife Regina*
have two children and live in a township outside
Durban, where he is employed in a carpet factory. In
a village two hours south of Durban, Shozi has
another wife and three children. He visits his
"country" family once a month.

Johannes Shozi walks with his three children and a family friend to their village home. Economic conditions in rural areas force large numbers of black men and women to seek work in urban areas. Most are prevented by law—and severe housing shortages—from bringing their families with them.

FACING PAGE: Shozi's "country" wife holds their youngest child while preparing tea. Electricity and running water in black rural areas are rarities.

PAGES 162 AND 163: Barend Bester, a laborer at Highveld Steel outside Johannesburg, stands in the foundry where molten steel is being poured. South Africa is a leading world producer of many minerals, including gold and manganese. Its steel industry employs more than 89,000 workers, and it produces 8.5 million tons of steel a year.

The newspaper banner outside a grocery store in the Orange Free State announces the extension of a State of Emergency first proclaimed in July 1985 and still in effect in 1988. Human rights organizations estimate at least 30,000 people have been detained without trial for varying periods under the Emergency's draconian provisions.

Pages 166 and 167: *Police raid a shebeen—or speakeasy—in a township outside the Orange Free State gold-mining town of Odendaalsrus and arrest one of the patrons. They claimed the man under arrest was obstructing police operations.*

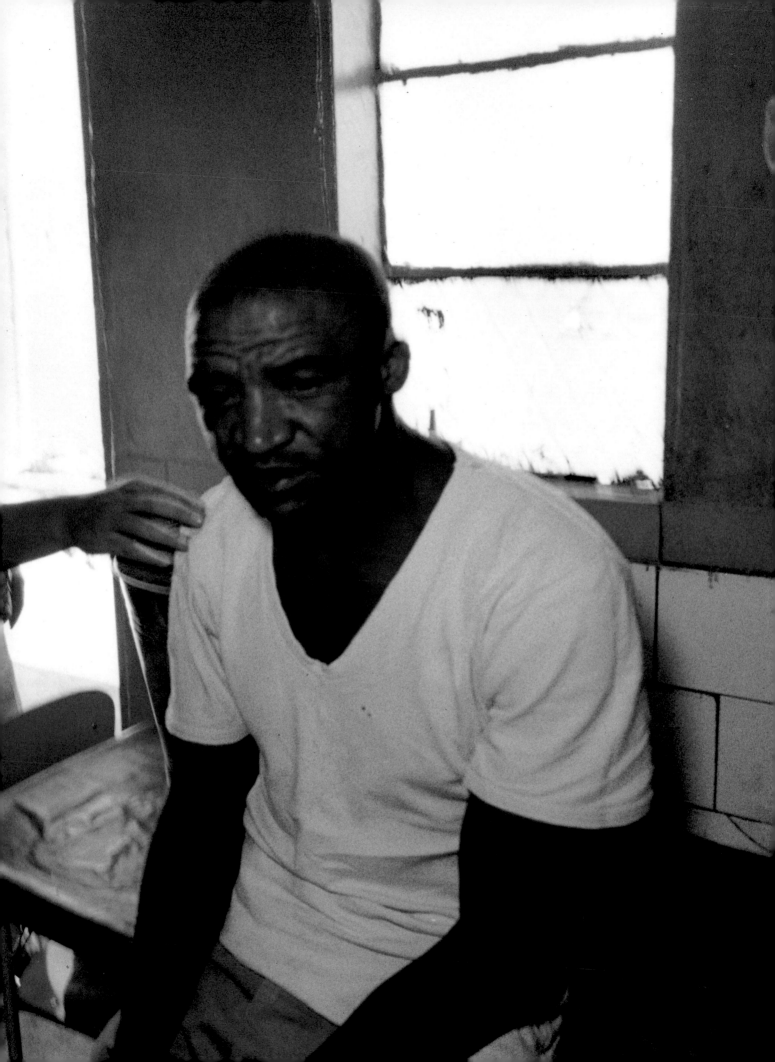

On a rare visit to a black township, Elise Botha, wife
of the President, gives candy to a patient at a
segregated hospital in Sebokeng, following the renewal
of the State of Emergency in 1985. Sebokeng, in the
Vaal triangle, was one of the first townships to erupt
in 1984 in a revolt over rents.

Frederick "Frikkie" Gerber, a Soweto township manager, accompanied by armed black constables, delivers an eviction notice to a rent striker at 4:00 A.M. Residents in townships around Johannesburg began a rent boycott in September 1984 as a form of protest against bad township services and apartheid. Soweto township officials estimate they are owed more than $60 million in back rent and utilities.

PAGES 170 AND 171: *Officials evict Sibongile Nkabinde from her Soweto home. She owed R1,001.49 (about $500.00) in rent and utilities.*

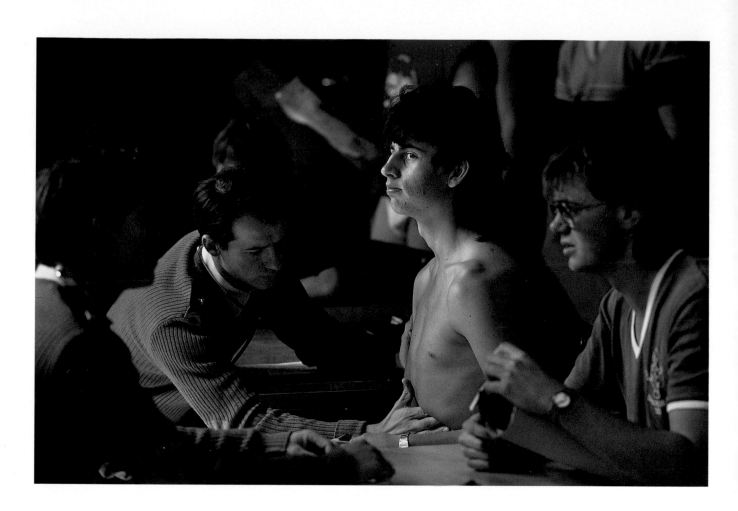

A nineteen-year-old youth begins his compulsory
military service with a medical examination. All
white men are now obliged to serve in the military for
two years and to attend annual training camps for an
additional twelve years.

PAGES 174 AND 175: *An instructor at the Soweto Township Police Training Academy who normally works as a desk officer was asked on this day by his brigadier to drill black trainee policemen. Township activists have targeted black policemen for their role in suppressing unrest: many have had their homes burned down and several have been killed. As a result, in most black townships the local police live in protected compounds.*

PAGES 176 AND 177: *The funeral procession for police officer Weyers Botha, one of three white policemen in their twenties killed in a car bomb blast outside the Magistrate's Court in Johannesburg in May 1987. Officer Botha's wife is in the car. The blast was blamed on the banned African National Congress.*

South African Defense Force soldiers march through central Johannesburg in a parade marking the city's centenary.

*Eugene Terre'Blanche, center, leader of the extreme
right-wing Afrikaner Weerstandsbeweeging (Afrikaner
Resistance Movement), leads prayers during an AWB
rally. As the government edges toward limited
reforms, right-wing groups opposed to any dilution of
apartheid are gaining adherents.*

An AWB ceremony near Dundee in Natal
commemorates the 1838 Battle of Blood River,
in which a Boer commando crushed the Zulu
battalions—known as impis—*of Chief Dingaan.*
It is not coincidental that the symbol on the flag
resembles a Nazi swastika; one of the tenets of the
AWB is white racial superiority.

Winnie Mandela, wife of the jailed African National Congress leader Nelson Mandela, who herself has gained national stature, is led by township youths to a funeral for unrest victims in Alexandra, outside Johannesburg.

Thousands of youths, known as comrades, jog through Atteridgeville township near Pretoria during a mass funeral.

*Rioting youths taunt soldiers in Gugulethu township
outside Cape Town.*

FACING PAGE: *A township youth stands ready, a
Molotov cocktail in hand. The whistle he wears is an
important means of street communication in a
township with few telephones.*

A crowd prepares to "necklace" a suspected police informant at a funeral in Duncan Village, outside East London. The necklace—a tire hung around the victim's neck, filled with gasoline, and set afire—was a popular method of execution during the height of the unrest, and the word has become part of the South African lexicon. Clergymen saved this man's life.

PAGES 186 AND 187: *During a funeral outside George, the Reverend Allan A. Boesak shields an accused police spy from a mob that most certainly would have killed him. Boesak is president of the World Alliance of Reformed Churches and a patron of the now-proscribed United Democratic Front, a broad alliance of opposition organizations.*

PAGES 188 AND 189: *Crowds lining the streets are reflected in the rear window of a hearse carrying relatives of a youth killed by riot police in Gugulethu outside Cape Town.*

PAGES 190 AND 191: *Coffins at an Alexandra township funeral are draped in the colors of the outlawed African National Congress. To defuse the political impact of funerals, police often use their powers under the Emergency to restrict the number of mourners and specify that coffins must be transported by car.*

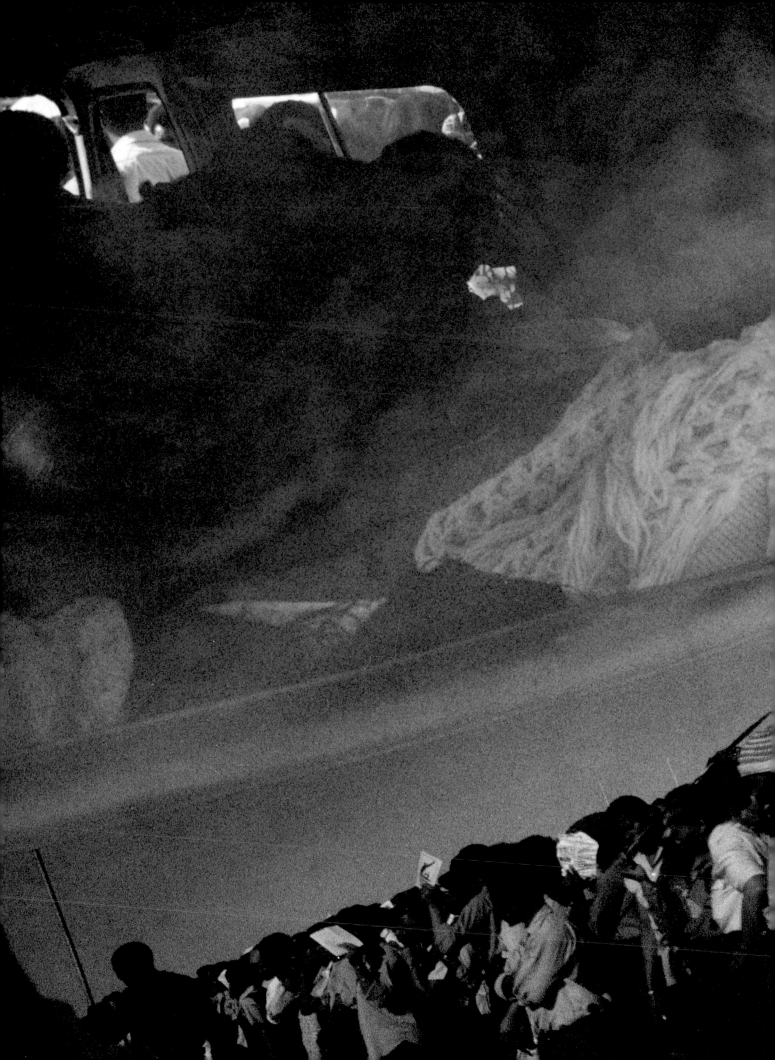

At a funeral in Alexandra township, a man covers the coffins of unrest victims with flags bearing the ANC's colors.

FACING PAGE: *Defiant mourners in Duncan Village, near East London. The Eastern Cape has long been one of the most volatile regions in the country and is the birthplace of many black leaders, including Steve Biko and Nelson Mandela.*

PAGES 194 AND 195: *Residents return from a funeral to Alexandra township. Much of the township has yet to be electrified, and the smoke of coal fires hangs like a pall over the houses, particularly in winter.*

PAGES 196 AND 197: *Winnie Mandela peers through bars on a protective gate that surrounds her home. She defied government orders banishing her to a remote township in the Orange Free State and returned to Soweto in 1985.*

PAGE 198: *Archbishop Desmond Tutu praying during a service at a Soweto church.*